This Great Game

This Great Game

A Rutledge Book

MAJOR LEAGUE BASEBALL

In association with The Benjamin Company, Inc.

Fred R. Sammis	Publisher
John T. Sammis	Creative Director
Doris Townsend	Editor-in-Chief
Allan Mogel	Art Director
Marilyn Weber	Managing Editor
Arthur Gubernick	Production Manager
Diane Matheson	Production Associate
Myra Poznick	Art Associate
Robert C. Shea	Associate Publisher

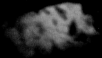

Contents

Baseball

a pictorial remembrance

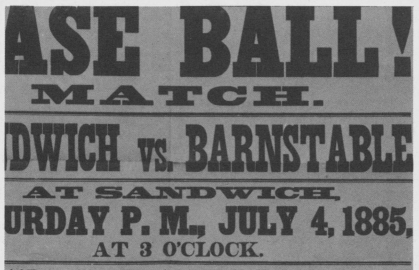

Baseball history seen through the camera's eye is as colorful as the record books are statistical, surprisingly as quaint and humorous as the common image: beer-in-the-bleachers or Ty Cobb with spikes. The nostalgia ranges from horse-and-buggy boundaries and hatted gentlemen spectators to old programs and a Hartnett slide at home.

Polo Grounds, 1890, when you brought your own bleacher seat.

The New York Highlanders play a 1907 game against Philadelphia to an Independence Day crowd that can't seem to get close enough to the action. Site is the Presbyterian Medical Center.

Gabby Harnett (5), 1922-1940 star, avoids Mickey Cochrane tag.

Yankee game in 1905. Insignia hasn't changed much.

Bases-loaded single at old Polo Grounds. Note how stadium changed from pages 10–11, how it changed again, pages 20–21.

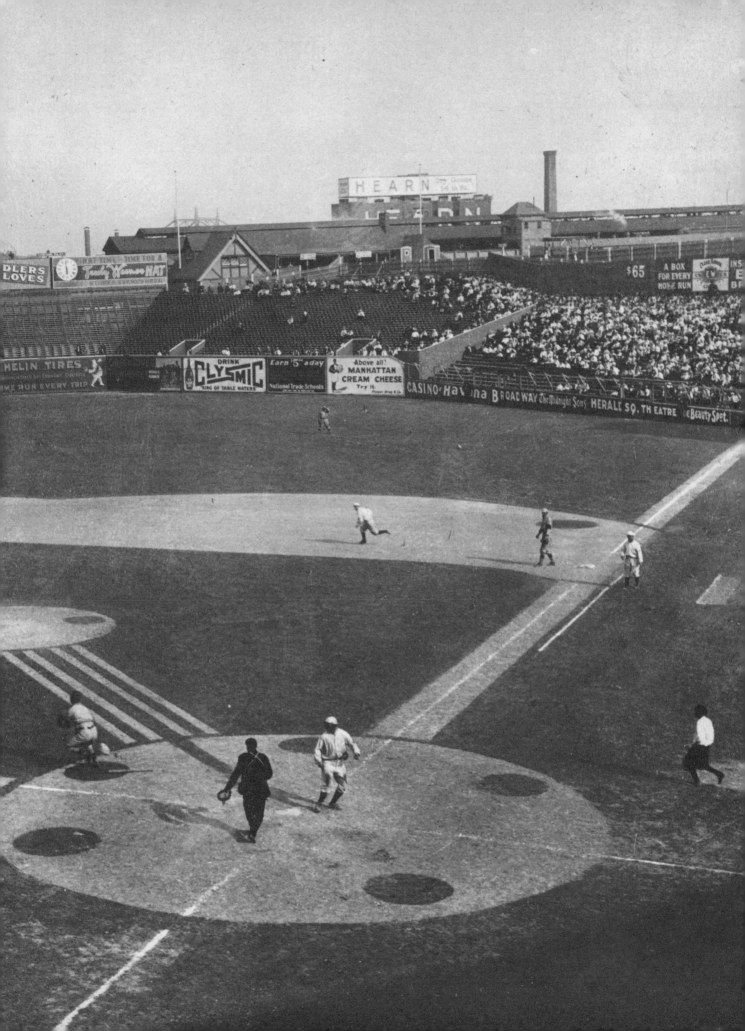

Babe Ruth skies one toward right. Yankees and Giants both used
Polo Grounds and vied for the World Series flag and prestige.

Fans, as they still do, swarm onto field after the game.

Baseball in the mind

---

by Roger Angell

"Here in the ball park, scattered across an immense green, each
player is isolated in our attention, utterly visible. Watch that
fielder just below us. Little seems to be expected of him: he
waits in easy composure, his hands on his knees, and when the
ball at last soars or bounces out to him, he seizes and dispatches
it with swift, haughty ease." Or is that only the mind's image?

Roger Angell, who views baseball with
compassion, admiration and understanding, is an
editor at *The New Yorker,* a writer of fiction, humor, sports and
editorial comment. He is the author of two books, *The Stone
Arbor* and *A Day in the Life of Roger Angell.*

There is a game of baseball that is not to be found in the schedules or the record books. It has no season, but it is best played in the winter, without the distraction of box scores and standings. This is the inner game, baseball in the mind, and there is no real fan who does not know it. It is a game of recollections, recapturings, and visions; figures and occasions return, enormous sounds rise and swell in our remembrance, and the interior stadium fills with light and yields up the sight of a young ballplayer, some hero perfectly memorized, just completing his own, unmistakable swing and now racing toward first—See the way he runs? Yes, that's him!—then leaning in as, still following the distant flight of the ball with his eyes, he takes his big turn at the base. Yet this is only the beginning, for baseball in the mind is not a mere yearning and returning. In time, this easy envisioning of restored players, winning hits, and famous rallies gives way to reconsiderations and reflections about the sport itself. By thinking about baseball like this, by playing it over and yet keeping it to ourselves, keeping it warm in a cold season, we begin to make discoveries. With luck, we may even penetrate some of its mysteries and learn once again how richly and variously the game can reward us.

One of those mysteries is vividness—the absolutely distinct inner vision we retain of that hitter, that eager base runner, who last played ball when we, too, were young. My father was talking the other day about some of the ballplayers he remembers. He grew up in Cleveland, and the Indians were his team. Still are. "We had Nap Lajoie at second," he said. "You've heard of him. A big broad-shouldered fellow, but a beautiful fielder. He was a rough customer. If he didn't like an umpire's call, he'd give him a faceful of tobacco juice. The shortstop was Terry Turner—a smaller man and blond. I can still see Lajoie picking up a grounder and wheeling and floating the ball over to Turner. Oh, he was quick on his feet! In right field we had Elmer Flick, now in the Hall of Fame. I liked the center fielder, too. His name was Harry Bay, and he wasn't a heavy hitter but he was very fast and covered a lot of ground. They said he could circle the bases in twelve seconds flat. I saw him get a home run inside the park—the ball hit on the infield and went right past the second baseman and out to the wall, and Bay beat the relay. I remember Addie Joss, our great southpaw. Tall, and an elegant pitcher. I once saw him pitch a perfect game. He died young."

My father has been a fan all his life, and he has pretty well seen them all. He has told me about the famous last game of the 1912 World Series, in Boston, when Fred Snodgrass dropped that fly ball in the tenth inning and the Red Sox scored twice and beat the Giants. I looked up Harry Bay and those other Indians in the Baseball Encyclopedia, and I think my father must have seen that inside-the-park homer in the summer of 1904. Lajoie batted .376 that year, and Addie Joss led the American League with an earned-run average of 1.59, but the Indians finished in fourth place. 1904. Sixty-seven years have gone by, but Nap Lajoie is in plain view and the ball still floats over to Terry Turner. Well, my father is eighty-one now, and old men are great rememberers of the distant past. But I am fifty, and I can also bring things back: Lefty Gomez, skinny-necked and frighteningly wild, pitching his first game at Yankee Stadium, against the White Sox and Red Faber in 1930. Old John McGraw, in a business suit and white fedora, sitting lumpily in a dark corner of the dugout at the Polo Grounds and glowering out at the field. Babe Ruth, wearing a new, bright-yellow glove, trotting out to right field, a swollen ballet dancer with delicate, almost feminine, feet and ankles. Ruth at the plate, uppercutting and missing, staggering with the force of his swing. Ruth and Lou Gehrig hitting back-to-back homers. Gehrig, in the summer of 1933, running bases with a bad leg in a key game against the Senators; hobbling, he rounds third, closely followed by young Dixie Walker, then a Yankee. The throw comes in to the plate, and the Washington catcher—it must have been Luke Sewell—tags out the sliding Gehrig and, in the same motion, the sliding Dixie Walker. A double play at the plate. The Yankees lose the game; the Senators go on to a pennant. And, back across the river again, Carl Hubbell. My own great southpaw, tall and elegant. Hub pitching: the loose motion; two slow, formal bows from the waist, glove and hands held almost in front of his face as he pivots, the long right leg (in long, peculiar pants) striding, and the ball, angling oddly, shooting past the batter. Hubbell walks gravely back to the bench, his pitching arm, as always, turned the wrong way round, with the palm out. Screwballer.

Any fan, as I say, can play this private game, extending it to extraordinary varieties and possibilities in his mind. Ruth bats against Sandy Koufax or Sam McDowell. . . . Hubbell pitches to Ted Williams, and the Kid, grinding the bat in his fists, twitches and blocks his hips with the pitch; he holds off but still follows the ball, leaning over and studying it like some curator as it leaps in just under his hands. . . . Why this vividness, even from an imaginary confrontation? I have watched many other sports, and I have followed some—football, hockey, tennis—with eagerness, but none of them yields these permanent interior pictures, these ancient and precise excitements. Baseball, I must conclude, is intensely remembered because only baseball is so intensely watched. The game forces intensity upon us.

Here in the ball park, scattered across an immense green, each player is isolated in our attention, utterly visible. Watch that fielder just below us. Little seems to be expected of him; he waits in easy composure, his hands on his knees, and when the ball at last soars or bounces out to him, he seizes and dispatches it with swift, haughty ease. It all looks easy, slow and, above all, safe. Yet we know better, for what is certain in baseball is that someone here, perhaps several people, will fail. They will be searched out, caught in the open and defeated, and there will be no confusion about it or a sharing of the blame.

This is sure to happen because what baseball requires of its athletes is, of course, nothing less than perfection, and perfection cannot be eased or divided. Every movement of every game, from first pitch to last out, is measured and recorded against an absolute standard, and thus each success is also a failure. Credit that

strikeout to the pitcher, but also count it against the batter's average; mark this run unearned, because the left fielder bobbled the ball for an instant and a runner moved up. Yet, faced with anxious loneliness, this sudden and repeated posing of danger, the big-league player defends himself with such courage and quick skill that the illusion of safety is sustained on the field. Tension is screwed tighter and tighter still as the moment of searching, the certain downfall, is postponed again and yet again, so that when disaster does come—a half-topped infield hit, a walk on a close three-and-two call, a low drive up the middle that just eludes the diving shortstop—we rise and cry out, for we have shared in something like a tragedy.

Televised baseball, I must add, does not seem capable of transmitting this emotion. Most baseball is seen on the tube now, and it is presented faithfully and with great technical skill. But we should remind ourselves of the limitations of the medium, which is irrevocably two-dimensional; even with several cameras, television cannot bring us the essential distances of the game— the simultaneous flight of a batted ball and its pursuit by the racing, straining outfielders, the swift convergence of runner and ball at a base. Foreshortened on our screen, the players on the field appear to be squashed together, almost touching each other, and watching them, we lose the sense of separateness and waiting that suggests the chilly private responsibilities of baseball.

This is a difficult game. It is so demanding that the best teams and the weakest teams can meet on almost even terms, with no assurance about the result of any one game. In March 1962, in St. Petersburg, the world champion Yankees played for the first time against the newly born New York Mets, one of the worst teams of all time, in a game that each team badly wanted to win; the winner, to nobody's real surprise, was the Mets. Last season the world champion Orioles won 108 games and lost 54; the lowest cellar team, the White Sox, won 56 and lost 106 games. This looks like an enormous disparity, but what it truly means is that the Orioles managed to win two out of every three games they played, while the White Sox won one out of three. That third game made the difference—and a kind of difference that can be appreciated when one notes that the season-long advantage that the White Sox gave up to all their opponents averaged out to 1.1 runs per game.

Team form is harder to establish in baseball than in any other sport, and the 162-game season not uncommonly comes down to October with two or three teams locked together at the top of the standings on the final weekend. Each inning of baseball's slow, searching time span, each game of its long season, is essential to the disclosure of its truths.

Form is the imposition of a regular pattern upon varying and unpredictable circumstances, but the patterns of baseball, for all its tautness and neatness, are never regular. Who can predict the winner and shape of today's game? Will it be a brisk, neat, two-hour shutout? An error-filled, languid 12–3 laugher? A riveting three-hour, fourteen-inning deadlock? What other sport produces these manic swings? For the players, too, form often undergoes terrible reversals; in no other sport is a champion athlete so often humiliated or a journeyman so easily exalted. The surprise, the upset, the total turnabout of expectations and reputations—these are delightful commonplaces of baseball. Al Gionfriddo, a part-time Dodger outfielder, stole second base in the ninth inning of the fourth game of the 1947 World Series to help set up Cookie Lavagetto's game-winning double (and the only Dodger hit of the game) off the Yankees' Bill Bevens. Two days later, Gionfriddo robbed Joe DiMaggio with a famous game-saving catch of a 415-foot drive in deepest left field at Yankee Stadium. Gionfriddo never made it back to the big leagues after that season.

Another irregular, the Mets' Al Weis, homered in the sixth and last game of the 1969 World Series, tying up the game that the Mets won in the next inning; it was Weis's third homer of the year and his first ever at Shea Stadium. Who remembers the second game of the 1956 World Series—an appallingly bad afternoon of baseball in which the Yankees' starter, Don Larsen, was yanked

after giving up a single and four walks in less than two innings? It was Larsen's *next* start, the fifth game, when he pitched his perfect game.

There is always a heavy splash of luck in these reversals. Luck, indeed, plays an almost predictable part in the game; we have all seen the enormous enemy clout into the bleachers that just hooks foul at the last instant or the half-checked swing that produces a game-winning blooper over second. Everyone complains about baseball luck, but I think it adds something to the game that is almost essential. Without it, such a rigorous and unforgiving pastime would be almost too painful to enjoy. Life, too, is altered by luck, and sometimes we recognize that luck, even when it is running against us, is almost a release, for it has excused us for a moment from pure responsibility.

No one, it becomes clear, can conquer this impossible and unpredictable game. Yet every player tries, and now and again, very rarely, we see a man who seems to have met all the demands, challenged all the implacable averages, spurned the mere luck. He has defied baseball, even altered it, and for a time at least, the game is truly his. One thinks of Willie Mays in the best of his youth, batting at the Polo Grounds, his whole body seeming to leap at the ball as he swung in an explosion of exuberance. Or Mays in center field, playing in so close that he appeared at times to be watching the game from over the second baseman's shoulder, and then that same joyful leap as he took off after a long, deep drive and ran it down, running so hard and so far that the ball itself seemed to stop in the air and wait for him.

One thinks of Jackie Robinson in a close game—any close game—playing the infield and glaring in at the enemy hitter, hating him and daring him, refusing to be beaten. And Sandy Koufax pitching in the last summers before he was disabled, in that time when he pitched a no-hitter every year for four years. Kicking swiftly, hiding the ball until the last instant, Koufax threw in a blur of motion, coming over the top, and the fast ball, appearing suddenly in the strike zone, sometimes jumped up so immoderately that his catcher had to take it with his glove shooting upward, like an infielder stabbing at a bad-hop grounder. I remember a batter taking a strike like that and then stepping out of the box for an instant and staring out at the pitcher with a look of utter incredulity—as if Koufax had just thrown an Easter egg past him.

Joe DiMaggio, batting, sometimes gave that same impression, the suggestion that the old rules and dimensions of baseball did not apply to him and that the game had at last grown unfairly easy. I saw DiMaggio once during his famous hitting streak in 1941; I'm not sure of the other team or the pitcher— perhaps it was the Tigers and Bobo Newsom —but I'm sure of DiMaggio pulling a line shot to left that collided preposterously with the bag at third base and ricocheted halfway out to center field. That record of hitting safely in fifty-six straight games seems as secure as any in baseball, but it does not awe me as much as the fact that DiMadge's old teammates claim that they *never* saw him commit an error of judgment in a ball game. Thirteen years and never a wrong throw, a cutoff man missed, an extra base passed up. Well, there was one time when he stretched a single against the Red Sox and was called out at second, but the umpire is said to have admitted later that he had blown the call.

And one more for the pantheon: Carl Yastrzemski. Yaz, to be precise, in September of the 1967 season, as his team, the Red Sox, fought and clawed against the White Sox and the Twins and the Tigers in the last two weeks of the closest and most vivid pennant race of our time. The presiding memory of that late summer is of Yastrzemski approaching the plate, once again in a situation where all hope rested on him, and settling himself in the batter's box—touching his helmet, tugging his belt, and just touching the tip of the bat to the ground, in precisely the same set of gestures— and then, in a storm of noise and pleading, swinging violently and perfectly . . . and hitting. In the last two weeks of that season Yaz batted .522—twenty-three hits for forty-four appearances, four doubles, five

home runs, sixteen runs batted in. In the final two games, against the Twins, both of which the Red Sox *had* to win for the pennant, he went seven for eight, won the first game with a homer, and saved the second with a brilliant, rally-killing throw to second base from deep left field. (He cooled off a little in the World Series, batting only .400 for seven games and hitting three homers.) Since then, the game and the averages have caught up with Yastrzemski, and he has never again approached that kind of performance. But then, of course, neither has anyone else.

Heroes, being exceptional, are always a distraction from more convoluted realities. To return to the game itself, we should look at baseball as it is actually played. We must select a particular game and reexamine it in box score and memory; only baseball, with its statistics and isolated fragments of time, permits so precise a reconstruction. Make it an important game: October 7, 1968, at Detroit, the fifth game of the World Series.

The fans are here—an immense noise, a cheerful, 53,634-man vociferosity, utterly fills the green, steep, high-walled box of Tiger Stadium. This is a good baseball town, and what binds this crowd together is not just the autumn occasion or hometown pride or even pride in the team, but another kind of warmth—a shared knowledge and intensity that quickens and deepens the afternoon's pleasure. But their cries have an anxious edge, too, for the Tigers are facing almost sure extinction. They trail the Cardinals by three games to one in the Series, and have never for a moment looked the equal of these defending world champions. Denny McLain, the Tigers' thirty-one game winner, was humiliated in the opener by the Cardinals' Bob Gibson, who set an all-time Series record by striking out seventeen Detroit batters. The Tigers came back the next day, winning rather easily behind their capable left-hander, Mickey Lolich, but the Cardinals demolished them in the next two games, scoring a total of seventeen runs and again brushing McLain aside; Gibson has now struck out twenty-seven

Tigers, and he will be ready to pitch again in the Series if needed. Even more disheartening is Lou Brock, the Cards' left fielder, who has already lashed out eight hits in the first four games and has stolen no less than seven bases; Bill Freehan, the Tigers' catcher, has a sore arm. And here, in the very top of the first, Brock leads off against Lolich and doubles to left; a moment later, Curt Flood singles and Orlando Cepeda homers into the left-field stands. The Tigers are down, 3–0, and the fans are wholly stilled.

In the third inning, Brock leads off with another hit, a single, and there is a bitter edge to the hometown cheers when Freehan, on a pitchout, at last throws him out, stealing, at second. There is no way for anyone to know, of course, that this is a profound omen; Brock has done his last damage to the Tigers in this Series. Now it is the fourth, and hope and shouting return. Mickey Stanley leads off the home half with a triple that lands, two inches fair, in the right-field corner. He scores on a fly. Willie Horton also triples. With two out, Jim Northrup smashes a hard grounder directly at the Cardinal second baseman, Julian Javier, and at the last instant the ball strikes something on the infield and leaps up and over Javier's head, and Horton scores. Luck! Luck twice over, if you remember how close Stanley's drive came to falling foul. But never mind; it's 3–2 now, and a game again.

But Brock is up, leading off once again, and an instant later he has driven a Lolich pitch off the left-field wall for a double. Now Javier singles to left, and Brock streaks around third base toward home. Bill Freehan braces himself in front of the plate, waiting for the throw; he has had a miserable Series, going hitless in fourteen at bats so far, and undergoing those repeated humiliations by the man who now races full speed at him, the man who must surely be counted, along with Gibson, as the Series hero. The throw comes in on the fly from Willie Horton in left, chest-high to Freehan; ball and base runner arrive together. Brock does not slide, and his left leg, the foot just descending on the plate, is banged away as he collides

with Freehan. Umpire Doug Harvey shoots up his fist: Out! It is a great play. Nothing has changed, the score is still 3–2, but everything has changed; something has shifted irrevocably in this game.

In the seventh inning, with one out and the Tigers still one run shy, Tiger manager Mayo Smith allows Lolich to bat for himself. Mickey Lolich has hit .114 for the season, and Smith has a pinch hitter on the bench named Gates Brown, who hit .370. But Lolich got two hits in his other Series start, including the first homer of his ten years in baseball. Mayo, sensing something that he will not be able to defend later if he is wrong, lets Lolich bat for himself, and Mickey pops a foolish little fly to right that falls in for a single. Now there is another single. A walk loads the bases, and Al Kaline comes to the plate. The noise in the stadium is insupportable. Kaline singles, and the Tigers go ahead by a run. Norm Cash drives in another. The Tigers win this searching, turned-about, lucky, marvelous game by 5–3.

Two days later, back in St. Louis, form shows its other face, as the Tigers rack up ten runs in the third inning and win by 13–1. McLain at last has his Series win. So it is Lolich against Gibson in the finale, of course. Nothing happens. Inning after inning goes by, zeros accumulate on the scoreboard, and anxiety and silence lengthen like shadows. In the sixth, Lou Brock singles. Daring Lolich, daring the nerves of the Tigers' infielders, openly forcing his luck, hoping perhaps to settle these enormous tensions and difficulties with one more act of bravado, Brock takes an enormous lead off first, draws the throw from Lolich, breaks for second, and is erased, just barely, by Cash's throw. A bit later, Curt Flood singles and he, too, is weirdly picked off first and caught in a rundown. Still no score. Gibson and Lolich, both exhausted, pitch on. With two out in the seventh, Cash singles for the Tigers' second hit of the day. Horton is safe on a slow bouncer that *just* gets through the left side of the infield. Jim Northrup hits the next pitch deep and high but straight at Flood, who is the best center fielder in the National League.

Flood starts in and then halts, stopping so quickly that his spikes churn up a green flap of turf; he reverses, now running madly toward the fence, and the ball sails over his head for a triple. Disaster. Suddenly, irreversibly, it has happened. Two runs are in, Freehan doubles in another, and two innings later the Tigers are Champions of the World.

I think I will always remember those two games, the fifth and the seventh, perfectly. And I remember something else about the the 1968 Series, when it was over—a feeling that almost everyone seemed to share: that Bob Gibson had not lost that last game, and that the Cardinals had not lost the Series. Certainly no one wanted to say that the Tigers had not won it, but there seemed to be something more that remained to be said. It was something about the levels and demands of the sport we had seen—as if the baseball itself had somehow surpassed the players and the results. It was the baseball that won.

Always, it seems, there is something more to be discovered about this game. Sit quietly in the upper stand and look at the field. Half-close your eyes against the sun, so that the players recede a little, and watch the movements of baseball. The pitcher, immobile on the mound, holds the inert white ball, his little lump of physics. Now, with abrupt gestures, he gives it enormous speed and direction, converting it suddenly into a line, a moving line. The batter, wielding a plane, attempts to intercept the line and acutely alter it, but he fails; the ball, a line again, is redrawn to the pitcher, in the center of this square, the diamond. Again the pitcher studies his task—the projection of his next line through the smallest possible segment of an invisible, seven-sided solid (the strike zone has depth, as well as height and width) sixty feet and six inches away; again the batter considers his even more difficult proposition, which is to reverse this imminent white speck, to redirect its energy not in a soft parabola or a series of diminishing squiggles but into a beautiful and dangerous new force, a force of perfect straightness and immense distance. In time, these and other lines

are drawn, there on the field; the batter and fielders are also transformed into fluidity, moving and converging, and we see now that all movement in baseball is a convergence toward fixed points—the pitched ball toward the plate, the thrown ball toward the right angles of the bases, the batted ball toward the as yet undrawn but already visible point of congruence either with the ground or a glove. Simultaneously, the fielders hasten toward that same point of meeting with the ball, and both the base runner and the ball, now redirected, race toward their encounter at the base. From our perch, we can sometimes see three or four or more such geometries appearing at the same instant on the green board below us and, mathematicians that we are, can sense their solutions even before they are fully drawn. It is neat, it is pretty, it is satisfying. Scientists speak of the profoundly moving esthetic beauty of mathematics, and perhaps the baseball field is one of the few places where the rest of us can glimpse this mystery.

The last dimension is time. Within the ball park, time moves differently, marked by no clock except the events of the game. This is the unique, unchangeable feature of baseball, and perhaps explains why this sport, for all the enormous changes it has undergone, remains somehow rustic, unviolent, and introspective. Baseball's time is seamless and invisible, a bubble within which players move at exactly the same pace and rhythms as their predecessors. This is the way the game was played in our youth and in our father's youth, and even back then, back in the country days, there must have been this same feeling that time could be stopped. Since baseball time is measured only in outs, all you have to do is succeed utterly; keep hitting, keep the rally alive, and you have defeated time. You remain forever young. Sitting in the stands, we sense this, if only dimly. The players below us—Mays, DiMaggio, Ruth, Snodgrass—swim and blur in memory, the ball floats over to Terry Turner, and the end of this game may never come.

No place to hide

an action portfolio

Clockwise from above: Herrmann stops Conigliaro; Dave Duncan directs play; Sanguillen grimaces at pop fly; Matty Alou breaks for third.

Left: Dalton Jones. Above: Billy Williams.

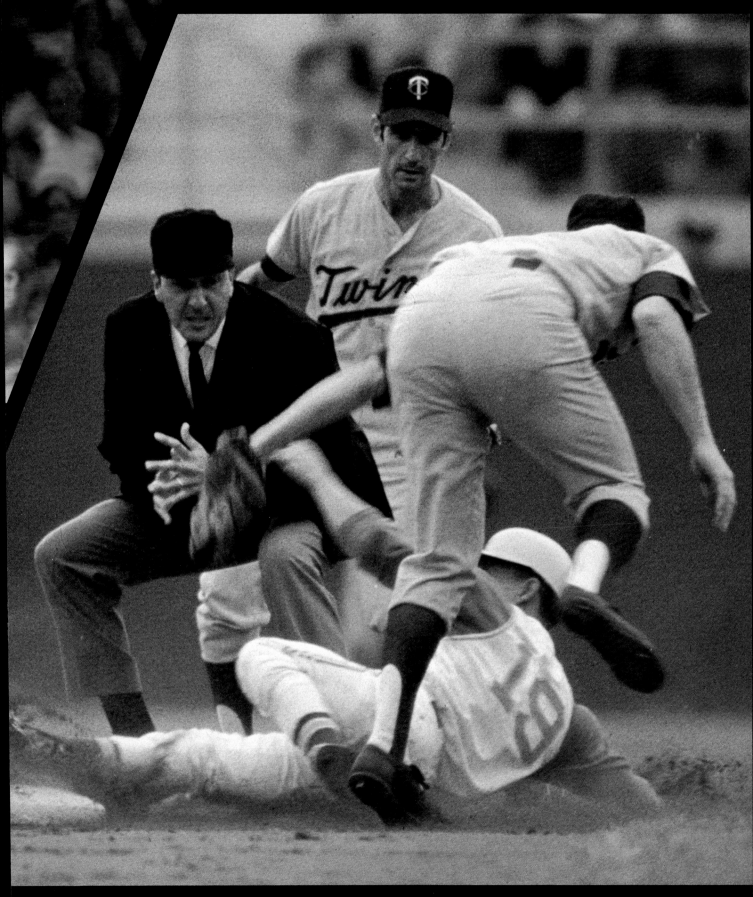

Clockwise from left: Perez fields a fair ball; Green completes double play; Howard rips one; Campaneris is caught stealing.

Brooks. Right: Woodward
avoids Blair slide.

Above: Cash turns double play over Bench.
Right: Campaneris nails Alomar.

A game of common sense

strategy and managing

by Earl Weaver

"You have to have a championship team to be a championship
manager." Whether or not this is a statement born of modesty is
a question left for the reader. Here Earl Weaver covers the art
of managing a ball club and the deployment of baseball strategy,
a subtle part of the game usually invisible to the onlooker.

Earl Weaver is the manager of the Baltimore Orioles, a club he
led to American League championships in 1969 and 1970. In
1970 the Orioles became World Champions. Mr. Weaver played
thirteen seasons of minor league ball (three MVP's, five times
fielding leader, five All-Star games) and managed minor league
ball clubs for twelve years before coming to the Orioles in
mid-1968. In thirteen full managerial seasons, his clubs have
finished first five times and second five times.

I think I went something like forty straight games last year with a different lineup each day. Most people would call that platooning. They can call it what they like. I call myself a statistics man.

At my request our front office keeps complete records. If we've got a game with the Yankees, before that game I'll sit at my desk with our lifetime stats versus whatever pitcher is going against us spread out in front of me. If Stan Bahnsen is throwing, for example, I'll have every statistic we've ever compiled against him. Whoever has batted well, say 10-for-36, against Bahnsen will bat up front. Frank Robinson will bat fourth since his record against Bahnsen is like .500 with power. If Mel Stottlemyre goes the next day, Boog Powell bats fourth for the same reasons. Frank will bat third or fifth depending on his average against Mel.

This theory holds true for me even if we've only faced a particular pitcher once. I feel once is better than no knowledge. If we have no batting record against a pitcher, then I go on whatever is known about him on past performances against other clubs. If he has trouble fielding bunts, or is not adept at holding runners on base, then my job is to get speed at the front of the lineup.

Let's take another example. Sam McDowell of the Indians is the pitcher against us. The previous day had Ellie Hendricks batting fifth, Mark Belanger eighth and Paul Blair second. Against McDowell, Andy Etchebarren will replace Hendricks, but probably won't bat fifth. Blair might fill that spot because I'll have moved Belanger up to second. Reason: We never score

well against McDowell, so we'll need to squeeze out the runs. One way is to bunt Don Buford to second whenever he gets on and Belanger is the man for that. Now, say we're in the ninth, two runs down, nobody on, the ninth spot due. I'll pinch-hit the man most likely to eke a hit off McDowell, hope Buford can get himself on, and then be in a position to pinch-hit power for Belanger, all because Mark was originally placed in the second spot. And against McDowell, there's a good chance we'll be two runs down going into the ninth.

Throughout the season, certain players, in fact all players, ideally, will need rest. The best place is a day game following a night

game, but I won't rest a man if he's got a good average against the scheduled pitcher. I'll wait until he's coming up against a guy he has trouble with. If Boog needs rest, I'll try to wait until we face somebody like the Twins' Jim Kaat no matter what the day. Then I'll replace him with Merv Rettenmund who hits Kaat pretty good.

In my book, the offense dictates over defense as to what players you're going to use during a certain game, and it also dictates rest periods. But sometimes you hurt

yourself too much by removing a player. That's why you'll hardly ever see Brooks Robinson rest, even though he needs it at times.

As far as a "game plan" is concerned, we have one to a certain extent. If a pitcher has a history of being wild early in the game, we'll start out by taking a lot of 2-1 pitches. But generally, our game plan is to lay back for four or five innings to see just what kind of game it's going to be. Our reasoning is that if you run early (say Blair steals if he gets on in the first inning and he's thrown out and Frank or Boog hits one out of the park), you've blown a chance to break open the game in the early stages.

But that's only a general game plan. Again, the pitcher will dictate what we do. If Minnesota's Dave Boswell is the pitcher, we know he has a good record of keeping the ball in the park. Frank or Boog probably aren't going to hit home runs anyway, so we may then decide to run early.

I've heard the Floyd Giebell story, which appears elsewhere in this book, about the time Giebell, a pitching rookie, was sacrificed against Bob Feller, so that neither of the two big guns had to pitch against Feller. I've only shifted my pitching rotation once. My pitchers like to pitch every fourth day. That's what they're grooved and conditioned to. They're not happy any other way and they don't pitch as well if I try to duck around some good opposition.

Actually, the one time I did change things around, I'm kind of

50

Above: Earl Weaver. Right: To prevent runner Pete Rose from getting too big a lead, Willie McCovey will signal his pitcher whether he is charging the sacrifice bunt or not.

pleased with. It happened during the 1970 season. We were in Detroit and Mike Cuellar was scheduled to start. The next day we were due in Baltimore to meet the Yankees in a two-game series. The Yankees had cut our lead from thirteen games to nine. Cuellar has an unbelievable record against the Yankees, so I decided I'd save Mike to open that series. Luckily, I got five-plus good innings from his replacement, Marcelino Lopez, and then brought in Dick Hall, who had an excellent record in relief against Detroit, which, of course, I knew before I made the pitching switch at the start of the game. Well, we won the Detroit game and Cuellar beat the Yankees the next day, 1–0, in ten innings.

Still, I hate to make changes like that and, as I've said, I've only done that once. The object is to win every game you play during the season. In order to do this you must try to win with every swing and every pitch.

Substitutions are dictated, as everything else seems to be, by the particular game in which you're playing. You start with the nine men you think are most able to win on that particular day. As the game progresses, you may have fallen behind and want to make a switch. For instance, we might be two or three runs behind and have gotten two men on base. Our batter may be Etchebarren or Belanger, neither of whom has a good long-ball record, especially against right-handers. We need a long ball. I substitute.

Or we might be ahead by a run in the late innings. For defensive purposes I might substitute

Rettenmund for Buford, not because Buford is a weak fielder, but because Merv is slightly better and I'm strengthening the team.

The hardest decision a manager must make is when to take out a pitcher. It's made on what you see and what you feel in your heart. Other elements enter in. Is your bullpen overworked? Are the relief men pitching well? What's your pitcher's history? A Cuellar or a Stottlemyre usually has trouble in the early going. You're reluctant to yank either one because he's having trouble in the first or second inning.

Take Mike Cuellar. He's thirty-four. He needs to break a sweat both to stay loose and to get his screwball working. In the first inning Brooks may make a diving catch, Belanger may go behind second to take away a single and Blair may go up against the wall to make a catch. One-two-three. But you know damn well Mike's going to be in trouble in the second. And you must allow for it.

The last game of the 1970 World Series is a perfect example. The temperature was in the low 70s, not hot enough for Mike. The sky was overcast. But it was humid. If Mike could make it through the first, he might break a sweat. The Reds scored two runs. Two men were out. Then a single scored a third run. Should I relieve Cuellar? Another run would kill us. But remember that the last run scored on a single—a good sign. Next, Tommy Helms was the batter, a good spray hitter, but not a power hitter. If Helms hit safely, it looked as if the worst shape we'd be in would be men on first and second or first and third. I'd still have a chance to go to the bullpen only three runs down. If the batter had been Johnny Bench, Tony Perez or Lee May I would have had to pull Cuellar. But I didn't. Mike retired Helms and came back to the dugout. The beads of perspiration on his forehead told me that if we could score, the Series was ours.

Carrying it just a bit further, if Cuellar gets in trouble in the second, then I have to pull him immediately. That's what happened in the second game of the Series. We were behind, Mike was having his usual early trouble, we were in the second inning. They had runners on and May was up. I couldn't take the chance of a long ball, so I pulled Mike.

Before the ball game starts is the time to think about your pinch hitters. Knowing who's available helps you determine your lineup. After the game gets under way, you look ahead again. If in the fifth inning it looks as if we might need a pinch hitter later, and that pinch hitter would seem to be either Curt Motton or Terry Crowley, I'll send both to the clubhouse to begin warming up, swinging bats. They'll be ready when I need them.

Some managers prefer an extra pitcher over a third-string catcher to complete their twenty-five-man team. Not me. Clay Dalrymple, a third-string catcher who comes to bat maybe only thirty times a year, is extremely valuable. His being there allows us to pinch-hit freely. Say we're in the seventh inning, needing runs. Men are on and Etchebarren is the hitter. They make a pitching change, bringing in a sidearming right-hander, which spells trouble for Andy. My ideal choice is Ellie Hendricks, our other catcher. With Dalrymple on the bench, I'm not hesitant to use Hendricks— without him I might balk at using my last catcher as a substitute. What happens if he gets hit with a foul tip and has to come out? In all probability we lose the ball game.

My philosophy on making substitutions, either pitching, hitting

*"Sometimes you've got to sacrifice
defensive ability for a man who
can pop the ball over the fence."*
Boog Powell sacrifices nothing.

or defensive, is that I'd rather lose a ball game by making a move than by just sitting on the bench and watching us blow it.

How important is a manager to a ball club? Very. I'm not saying that just because I have pride in my job. A manager has a lot of things to do right. It's not easy. By the same token, you don't have to be a genius to play baseball. If you've thought out the situation before it occurs, common sense should dictate the move you then make. That applies, incidentally, to managers and players alike.

To illustrate, I point to a game when I was managing at Rochester. We were in the bottom of the ninth, we had the bases full and there was one out in a tie ball game. I was in the third-base coaching box, where managers were at times in the minor leagues. The batter hit a short fly to left, so I quickly ordered the runner, Mickey McGuire, to try to draw a throw. The ball wasn't hit deeply enough to score, but I figured there was always a chance for a wild peg.

McGuire, as instructed, took eight or ten steps down the line, stopped and headed back, drawing a throw home. He also, however, drew the runner from second, who was tagged out sliding into third. Inning over. Their first man in the tenth hit a homer and we failed to score in our half.

My point: If that runner on second had taken a moment ahead of time to think out the situation, common sense would have dictated that he remain on second. If McGuire runs, which my man at second must have thought he was doing, and he's out, the inning is over. If he's safe, the game is over. It was one of the few

times in baseball the runner could (and should) have just stood around and watched the play.

It's my belief that all managers in the big leagues today have the ability to run a ball club. One thing that separates the good from the herd is the ability to show judgment in selecting a team during spring training and by trading.

Once you've got a ball club, it's the manager's job to use his men to the best of their abilities and to recognize their incapabilities.

Don't yell at a guy if he's too slow going from first to third on a single. If he is competent in all other phases of the game, don't harass him. Talk to him, but recognize his lack—or compensate. On my club, Brooks Robinson is probably the slowest man from home to first. If I want him in my lineup, I've got to recognize that he's going to hit into a certain number of double plays during the course of the season. But I can help the situation by placing fast men ahead of him or by running the man at first when Brooks comes to bat.

When I go to spring training I'm given forty men to work with,

twenty-five of whom come back north with the club. These forty men have been chosen mainly by the general manager on advice from me and the rest of the organization. Occasionally we'll have a few more than forty, those extras usually being batting-practice pitchers who can use the work. Steve Barber was one of those extras one year and went on to become Baltimore's first twenty-game winner.

During the winter I tell the guys to keep loose. For the men around the Baltimore area we have regularly scheduled basketball games and workouts. For the others, we send them a printed exercise schedule. We do this partly as a result of the 1967 season. In 1966 we won the World Series in four straight over the Dodgers. Our big guns on the mound were Wally Bunker, Dave McNally and Jim Palmer, all young pitchers. The next season all three came up with sore arms and we tied for sixth. So now my pitchers work out during the winter, staying loose. When they arrive at spring training they can throw seven to ten minutes the first day. In addition, they run. Before the season starts they have built up their arms and legs to a point where any one of them will be able to throw from 100 to 160 pitches a game from opening day on.

A common misconception is that ballplayers have a two- to three-hour job. In truth, they arrive at the ball park at 3:30 or 4 for an 8 P.M. start. They've got to start working, loosening up. During a ball game there's a lot of relative inactivity when muscles tighten up. Rain produces a million muscle pulls. And if you're tight, you've got a good chance of really hurting yourself, probably more so than if you were loose and got involved with one of the three big dangers

55

Left: Manager Rigney confers with catcher George Mitterwald and Jim Perry. Whether to bring in a new pitcher is a tough decision. Above: Reds' Sparky Anderson.

Willie Mays catches his spikes, a common cause of injury.

of the sport: catching spikes on a slide, running into the wall, getting hit by a pitch.

I tell everybody at the start of spring training that there are twenty-five positions to fill, so work your hardest. The veterans on my ball club know better. They know that simply on the basis of past performance, they'll be going north and will stay at least through the first few weeks of the season. The big reason I let the vets know they've got a job is so they won't do something foolish in an effort to beat out a hot rookie. I don't want my established ballplayers diving into second base or hanging over the plate against a wild kid on the mound who is trying to impress us with his speed. Early injuries can be fatal to a ball club.

Batting practice is important for both pitchers and hitters. Pitchers need to get control throwing off a mound. The batters need to strengthen their wrists and arms. During spring training, my men take ten swings, run the bases and return to their group of six or seven to hit again. This process is repeated six or seven times. In the meantime, other groups are shagging flies, working double plays and so forth.

In addition to batting practice and shagging balls, we work on plays as a team (defense against a bunt, defense against certain players, stealing, double steals, breaking up double steals and so forth). You must perform these plays properly if you're going to win your share of one-run games. My figures may be slightly off, but I think our record last year in one-run games was 41-15. If we had only played .500 ball in those games, our record would have been 27-27 and the flag goes to the Yankees.

When selecting my twenty-five men, I try to keep the club level in all departments. I look for speed from first to third, defense (which is born into players), pitching (I try to find four men who can give the club from 250 to 300 innings a

58

Clockwise from left: Clay Carroll squares around perfectly; Brooks Robinson calls for the bunt and fields it flawlessly; Bert Campaneris bunts for a hit.

season) and power (sometimes you've got to sacrifice defensive ability for a man who can pop the ball over the fence). Clete Boyer might have had trouble staying with a club that was in need of power. But he played for the Yankees, a club that was well balanced, and he became a standout third baseman.

Most managers try to put their power at the corners (left field, right, first and third). Fewer balls are hit to the corners. I don't try to place power behind the plate. The catcher is in on every play. It's more important for him to be good defensively. Of course, there are always exceptions. Yankee Stadium's left field goes back 460 feet. You don't find many so-so left fielders playing for the Yanks. And there's always Clete Boyer. Again, he played the corner and had little power. But Mickey Mantle and Roger Maris supplied all the

power the Yankees ever needed. And so they balanced with exceptional defense.

I hate to let a starting pitcher, from the seventh inning on, throw to the winning run. This, of course, doesn't apply to one-run games, where, if a man singled or walked, the next man up would be the winning run. But if we're in the seventh two runs up and our pitcher has worked hard and two men get on, then I won't let him work to the winning run at the plate. As a result of this philosophy I've graciously been given the nickname "Captain Hook."

I remember once we were playing the Yankees in the Stadium. It was the first game of a doubleheader. Palmer was pitching. We were ahead 4–2 in the ninth. They got a man on, then Jim retired two, but then they got another man on. Everything was ripe for me to take Jim out. Not only was he obviously

tiring, but Jake Gibbs was the batter, a left-handed pull hitter in a stadium with the shortest right-field fence down the line. But for some crazy reason I decided to let Jim continue. Conscious of the home-run situation, he worked too cautiously and walked Gibbs.

Then I made the move, obviously too late. Pete Richert got the job of pitching to Roy White, who probably hasn't made the last out of any ball game he's ever played in. White singled for two runs. Richert struck out the next man, Bobby Murcer, on three pitches, but we lost the game in the fourteenth. After the game Palmer kidded me. "What's the matter, Captain, get polio?" That shook me up so much that Ralph Houk and I ended up using twenty-one pitchers during both games of the doubleheader.

Although there are definitely times when the sacrifice can be the most important play in baseball, I

believe that generally it is an overrated move. Statistics show that a man on first with nobody out has a better chance of scoring than a man on second does with one out. And a man on second with nobody out has a better chance of scoring than a man on third with one out. But of course, the individual situation—as always—dictates the correct move. Let's take two examples:

First, when the chances seem less in favor of the man at bat advancing the runner, the sacrifice may be in order. A .220 hitter, for instance, or the pitcher whose average usually ranges from .050 to .150.

On the other hand, let's say the Orioles have a man on first and one out. My next two batters are Frank Robinson and Boog Powell. Certainly, Frank is not going to be sacrificing to get a man in scoring position with Boog coming to bat.

Remember, Boog is going to be walked with first base open. What I'd be doing would be to give up an out without my two best hitters even getting a swing at the ball. And I'd have given up a good chance for a home run. You get only three outs an inning, so why give any away if you can avoid it?

The same man who came up with those scoring statistics also decided that you should place your highest average hitter first, your next highest average hitter second, and so on down the line. That only works if you've got nine high average hitters. What about a game in which you're going against an exceptional pitcher and you know you must squeeze out runs? If your lead-off man gets on, you certainly wouldn't want your second-best hitter bunting. You'd be wasting him. Instead, you'd want a bunter up there, or a man who can hit behind a runner.

Much of what a manager teaches, and much of baseball strategy, revolve around baserunning and preventing baserunning. How much can a runner really do out there? For instance, take a situation in which there's a runner on second, nobody out. The hitter is a faster base runner than the man on second. The ball is hit on the ground in front of the base runner. This particular base runner sizes up the situation and decides to go, breaking one of baseball's so-called cardinal rules (you don't run on a ball hit in front of you if you don't have to). But this runner gets himself in a rundown, purposely, giving the batter enough time to get to second. The situation is the same as if he hadn't run—a man on

Robinson, a man who gets little rest, robs the Reds of another hit during the 1970 World Series.

second, one out. But now the faster
runner is in scoring position.

Fine in theory. But don't forget
that the offense must be aware of
the defensive potential. Such a
situation would not be possible
against the Orioles. If that runner on
second tried to get into a rundown,
he'd find himself tagged out long
before the hitter could get to
second, and if the hitter tried to
make second, he'd be doubled up.
It's our belief that it only takes
one throw to complete a rundown.
We teach this in spring training as
one of the fundamentals vital to
learn if a team is to be a pennant
contender.

The more an infield can work
together, the better off the team
will be. We're fortunate in having
an infield that has been intact since
1967. It's so often the little things
that count. If your infield is deficient
in a seemingly minor execution,
such as taking three or four throws
to eliminate a runner in a rundown,
that could be just the difference
between winning a pennant and
coming in second. And if you're
deficient in more than one of these
aspects, who knows how many
games those "little things" can cost
the club? I know that when we
don't execute a play correctly,
we're out on the field early the next
morning practicing until we get it
right. I don't care how long a fellow
has played in the major leagues or
how much he thinks he knows. He's
going to do any particular phase of
the game the way I want it done.

Let's talk about other strategic
situations. Suppose the opposition
has runners on first and third. They
try the double steal. Now there's an
old misconception that if the ball,
thrown by the catcher, gets through
to the second baseman or the
shortstop, then the runner at third
should be able to score. No way,
not if the catcher takes a short
glance at the runner coming down
the line before he releases the ball.
That short glance should stop the
runner's progress (if it doesn't, he'll

Clockwise from below: Rick Monday on a hit-and-run; Paul Blair, rounding second, can make home on a single; runner gets go-ahead from third base coach's signal.

63

sacrifice bunt pushed down the first base line could always advance him to second. Now, however, the first baseman has a signal option with his pitcher. He can fake his charge to home with two or three quick steps, then hustle back to the bag. The pitcher will not deliver to the plate, but throw instead to first. As a result, the runner can't be sure when the first baseman really is going to the plate and, therefore, he can't get those extra two steps that guarantee his making second.

As in the more obvious defensive alignments in football, such as when linebackers fake a blitz or when defensive backfield men switch from zone to man-to-man coverage, defense in baseball should be designed to create confusion for the offense. Take an instance in which there are men on first and second and the pitcher is at bat. Obvious bunt situation. Old theory would assure a successful advancement of runners. If, the theory states, you bunt hard enough down the third-base line, the third baseman will have to field it. With nobody covering third, the runner or runners safely advance.

Now, that play can be defensed. For instance, the third baseman can charge hard, the shortstop can cover third, the second baseman will cover second and the first baseman will stay at first while the pitcher covers the first-base line. The result can be either a 5-6-3 or a 5-4-3 double play, depending on how the third baseman, on instructions from the catcher, decides to play it.

Or, it can be worked the opposite way, with the first baseman

be thrown out). Once the runner has hesitated, I don't care how fast he is, there's no way he's going to beat a thrown ball to short or second back to the plate.

What about that runner at first? Haven't you given him a better chance of stealing by first taking that extra second to look down to third? Sure. But remember, only a fast man will be sent to second to work the double steal. And fast men steal second better than 60 percent of the time they try. Since the chances are they're going to steal successfully anyway, you're really not giving up that much to begin with. In addition, you've prevented a run from scoring.

Another theory disappearing from the game is the automatic use of the sacrifice bunt, but not for the reasons I mentioned earlier. It used to be that with a runner on first, a

Above: Jim Palmer, a victim of a sore arm in 1967, is now counted on to supply Orioles with 250–300 innings a season. Right: Coach Staller calls for bullpen help.

charging, the third baseman hanging back, the second baseman covering first, the shortstop going to second and the pitcher covering the third-base line. A third option might be for both third baseman and first baseman to charge while the shortstop sneaks in behind the runner, hopefully with a big lead, for a pick-off play. It all depends on the signal given by, in our case, third baseman Brooks Robinson. (If I don't approve of his signal, I'll whistle out there and change it.) The long-range result is that the batter must guess which way to bunt the ball. (Next year, I suppose, we'll have to let somebody else call the signals. After what I've said here everybody will be watching Brooks.)

The point is, each additional year baseball is played there are more deviations from basic defensive formations. As a result, the sacrifice is less and less a good bet.

Offensively, there's one type of baserunning you can't teach. I'm talking about instinctive base-running. The Orioles have two such instinctive runners in the Robinsons, each in his own way.

Frank is one of the most amazing base runners I've ever seen. I remember a situation something like the one we've just discussed. Paul Blair was on second, Frank was hitting. The ball was hit in front of Paul and, misjudging it, he ran for third. He realized his mistake soon enough to allow himself to be caught in a rundown. Well, first the defense got itself all tangled up. The first baseman backed up the shortstop, the second baseman backed up the third baseman, the pitcher backed somebody else, the catcher backed up the backed-up third baseman. Four throws later, Frank was standing on second watching the action.

Their catcher by then had the

Clockwise from above: Ted Williams, Washington's teacher-manager; Weaver, a stickler for the rule book, argues his point; Frank Robinson gives a reprimand.

67

ball. All he had to do now was casually to trot Blair back to second, where he'd be able to take his choice of runners to tag. But Frank was a step ahead of that thought process and, as the catcher went after Blair, he broke *back* to first. The catcher, startled, hesitated just long enough to allow Blair to slide safely into second while Frank jogged unopposed back to first.

When Frank is up with either Buford or Blair on first, and the outfield is playing him the way it usually does—pulled to left—he'll hit to right. Rounding first, and while the right fielder is catching up with the ball, Frank will time his run so that the outfielder will be seduced into throwing to second, probably in time to get Frank. But in the meantime, Buford or Blair can make it home. And often, because the first baseman is usually in to take the cutoff throw, Frank will be able to stop and get back to first.

As for Brooks, he may be the slowest man on the Orioles, but he's the fastest between first and third. He has lined up where those outfielders are, and at the crack of the bat seems to know whether or not the ball will be caught. He'll be rounding second while another player would be halfway between bases waiting to see where the ball was going to land.

These are really examples of thought-out plays combined with instinct. There are a number of plays similar to these that a team can develop and use successfully during the season. But since I'm staying in the American League next year, I won't go into them.

Baseball, while being a team sport, is also a highly individual sport. If all nine men have a good day as individuals, then the team will look good as a whole. And because baseball is so statistically oriented, the concept of team play becomes one of sacrifice.

The most obvious example is

the situation in which you have a man on second, nobody out. As we discussed, probability percentages suggest you take your three shots at scoring him from second. But while you're at it, why not try to hit to right? That way, on an out, you can be sure to advance the runner. Hell, your best hitters only hit approximately three out of ten times up. So why not try going to right? Furthermore, if your big hitters do something like that, it sets an example for the younger players. That, to me, is

what makes baseball a team sport.

Let's talk a moment about the squeeze play. Some people think that whenever a man gets to third with fewer than two outs, you should guarantee yourself a run by using a suicide, or semi-suicide, squeeze bunt. First of all, with a man on third and fewer than two outs, you've got a good chance of going on to bigger and better things than a one-run inning. And during the first half of a ball game, that's important.

Secondly, to guarantee a run,

From left: Jim Maloney, well protected, throws some batting practice; Mike Cuellar struggling in the early innings; Willie Mays takes a few practice swings.

you've got to be sure of bunting the ball, and bunting it downward. To do that the batter has to square around. Many batters are afraid of the pitch in that position. Others have trouble with the curve and find themselves lunging after the ball too late. In addition, there's the matter of timing. If the batter squares too early, he'll get the ball thrown behind his neck. If he squares too late, he'll be in a bad bunting stance.

The best time to use a squeeze, then, is late in a game when one run can mean the ball game and when your batter is a man who strikes out a lot.

Without coaches, a manager would be hard pressed to do any kind of a respectable job. On the baselines, they have important assignments. Being a third-base coach is probably the hardest job in baseball. Not only do you have to answer for your own misjudgments, but also for the mistakes of the players who fail to heed your signs. The first-base coach has a more subtle job. First, he must keep the base runner in the game. Second, he must act as a sign stealer. He watches the pitcher for giveaways or an exposed ball, he eyes the catcher and he constantly is alert to dugout signs.

I think the best coach is a man who wasn't a star in his day— guys like myself and George Bamberger, our pitching coach. We more or less existed on what we could learn about the game. Guys like Bob Feller or Hal Newhouser with a fantastic fast ball or a great curve, would, to my mind, not make as ideal a coach as a Bamberger who, to survive in the majors, had to rely on sliders, screwballs, changes and spot pitching.

Coaches must be tough. They cannot allow loafing during practice sessions. And they must have the ability to impart their knowledge to the players. You can't coach if you can't get a man to accept what you're saying.

When picking a coaching team you go for a well-rounded staff. I've got Billy Hunter for the infield and for his ability to take over workouts, thus freeing me to talk individually to the ballplayers. I've got George Staller for outfield and hitting, Bamberger for pitching and Jim Frey for the bullpen. (Frey, among other things, is a good disciplinarian—and that's important out there.)

A common question among baseball fans is what percentage of the game is pitching, what hitting and how much defense. I feel pitching is 90 percent of the game. I suppose that percentage changes according to certain situations, but pitching certainly initiates every play, and to that extent everything depends on it. The object of the game is to outscore the opposition. If you have a man on the mound who can keep men off the bases, you'll win. Naturally, defense contributes.

Take Cuellar again. He's cold in the first inning. The first man singles. The next batter hits a shot down to third that Brooks turns into a double play. The next two men single and the third sends Blair against the wall to make the catch. No runs. In the second game of the Series in which I yanked Cuellar, he would have been out of the inning with no runs had Belanger not made an error.

The most important thing a pitcher can do, then, is to keep the ball inside the park. Look at the 1969 World Series. The Mets' pitchers kept the ball this side of the fence. Guys like Tommie Agee and Ron Swoboda did the rest, Swoboda's catch being one that no baseball fan will ever forget. But the point is, the pitchers kept the ball where their fielders could get at it.

It's a funny thing about the World Series. You get anxious. In 1969 we really wanted at those Mets' pitchers. As a result, we swung at 2-0 pitches. Their pitchers hung tough, kept the ball low and aimed for the corners. If we had taken, the worst it could have been was a 2-1 count. But instead, we grounded out. In the 1970 Series we were more selective. By waiting for our pitches, we hit home runs, and therein lies the difference. In two games against Cincinnati, we hit three home runs. Three was our entire total against the Mets. The Mets beat us four games to one; we beat the Reds by the same margin.

Managing is a tough job. You're dealing with men but playing a game. How do you handle the players? First of all, you have team rules, rules that apply to everybody no matter who they are, no matter what they've accomplished. If you set a 1 A.M. curfew before a day game, you can't allow a ten-year man to come in at 2 A.M. The same rules apply for reporting to the ball park. If you fail in this department, the result is resentment.

Naturally, there are exceptions. If a man like Frank Robinson, who knows himself, comes to me and complains of the heat, saying he would like to skip batting practice, that's OK. And if Frank's in a hitting streak, he'll skip practice to conserve energy for the game. But if he's in a slump, he's out at the park two hours early, working in the batting cage.

Certainly a manager can't be buddy-buddy with his players. Friendship leads to a hesitancy to make a move. Although I must know all my players' faults on the field, I certainly don't want to know what they are off the field. That works both ways. A manager must have the respect of his players. I sure as hell don't want them to know all my little idiosyncrasies.

At the same time, the last thing I want is for the guys to feel I'm remote, hard to reach. It's not going to help a player who feels he shouldn't be on the bench to complain to the man sitting next to him. On our team, if a man has a complaint, he comes to me with it and we hash it over in the privacy of my office.

I have a philosophy of life that may or may not have anything to do with being a decent manager. I feel that anything within the realm of a man's imagination is within the realm of possibility. I know when I was a kid my dream was someday to be in the World Series. When I became a ballplayer I survived by doing the little things, such as hitting to right, bunting, grabbing another base—but it became apparent soon enough that I wasn't going to get myself into the World Series as a player. Yet I never gave up my dream. And I did make it to the Series.

Finally, there's no way a guy can be a championship manager unless he has a contending team. In fact, you might almost say he has to have a championship team. I don't know what that may say about me as a manager, but—hell, baseball's just a game of common sense, anyway.

The salaried elite

by Douglass Wallop

"Baseball has a way of opening doors," writes Douglass
Wallop. It opened the door to Jackie Robinson at a time when
nobody else would. It allows a person born of the ghetto to
earn an annual salary of $150,000. But while it can be said that
great players make great salaries, it cannot be said in reverse.
The men who make great salaries earn them. Six such men
from each league have been selected for portrayal by Mr.
Wallop and painter LeRoy Neiman.

Douglass Wallop has written nine novels, among them
The Year the Yankees Lost the Pennant, which became the
smash Broadway musical *Damn Yankees.* Other novels
include *One Stone* and *The Good Life,* the latter scheduled this
year as a television pilot. His single book of non-fiction is
Baseball: An Informal History.

Frank Robinson, writing of his father, recalls: "He certainly was not a real father to me. I don't think anyone can be a real father when he doesn't spend any time at home with his family. But he would come around every now and then after he left home. I remember he taught me how to tie my shoes, and he would give me rewards for counting from one to a hundred and things like that."

To the young Frank Robinson, one of ten children living out a deprived childhood in black Oakland, the world could not have seemed a promising place, but in Robinson's future there was a shower of gold. Since the days when he learned to tie his shoelaces under the eye of a sometimes-father, the rewards have been prodigious. It is said that each year he counts them in thousands of dollars, from one to a hundred and beyond.

Rising from a meager childhood to the economic aristocracy is one of the fundamentals of the American dream. The dream still comes true and perhaps nowhere more dramatically than in sports. Baseball has been called the national folk drama and Americans, a ball-playing audience, seem to take for granted the huge salaries paid to the talented stars who act out fantasies for them down on the playing field. Babe Ruth, who spent his boyhood in a Baltimore orphanage, went on with his mighty bat and flamboyant ways to pull down a greater salary than the then President of the United States—$80,000 to Cal Coolidge's $75,000—

and although at the time the nation was awed, it was a sort of self-awe and even pride that we should be such a strange, prodigal people, paying a pudgy out-fielder with dainty legs more money than the President.

For his day, the Babe's $80,000 was astronomical, in a class by itself. Today's moneyed elite count their salaries in six figures, which, of course, does not mean that today's elite are all as talented as Ruth nor even as talented as other stars of an earlier time. Among those, for example, who never earned $100,000 are Ty Cobb, Rogers Hornsby, Lou Gehrig, Jimmy Foxx and, for that matter, the Babe himself. Since it is clumsy if not impossible to compare era with era, all that can be said for certain is that today's larger salaries are a reflection of the changed value of the dollar, a by-product of inflation and of profits padded by television, although there is as well some indication of a change in owner-attitudes. Once the $100,000 salary barrier was broken, some owners seemed to find it a thrill to let the world know that they too had on their rosters a $100,000 ballplayer, viewing it as a mark of prestige even though it meant cash out of pocket. (Others, more restrained, have managed so far to forgo both the thrill and the prestige.)

In any appraisal of what admits a player to the blue-ribbon salary class, therefore, his owner's willingness to pay cannot be disregarded, nor is it possible to overlook certain colorful qualities that give some players a crowd appeal above and beyond their merit as performers. Hence, by the test of time, the mere fact of a high salary does not automatically mean historical excellence, nor for that matter does it automatically qualify a player for selection to the gallery of twelve here depicted. The makeup of any such gallery is, of course, open to argument and in picking the twelve—six players from each league—it has been necessary to be arbitrarily selective. Those chosen combine a high order of talent, day-in day-out performance, value to their respective teams and endurance over long careers. When the composite of these qualities seemed approximately equal, the higher-paid player was selected.

Among the elite there are a few who, along with their huge salaries, have also earned illustrious places in baseball history. Most notable of these is Willie Mays, of Alabama, New York and California—where he is still on view—a baseball classic, a legend still playing ball.

There was a time in an earlier rural America when the big-league star most often came from the farm or hamlet. Willie Mays, son of an Alabama sharecropper, may turn out to have been not only the foremost, and one of the first, of the black players to make it big, but also one of the last of the farm boys.

Because of the race bias that so long prevailed, major-league baseball was deprived of Josh Gibson and the best of Satchel Paige, but it was not, thank God, deprived of Willie Mays. As a teen-ager, Willie played

for the Birmingham Black Barons, and if the color line had still been drawn, he would have played out his days in the Negro leagues. But by then Branch Rickey and Jackie Robinson had opened the gates, and in 1951 Willie joined the New York Giants and baseball has been richer ever since. In a decade when the three New York teams dominated the game, in an era of New York heroes, Willie was a super-hero, and when the Giants moved to the opposite coast and became the Giants of San Francisco, Willie moved with them to begin a second decade of blazing stardom. For twenty seasons he has been the complete ballplayer, doing more things well than either Cobb or Ruth, and adding the defensive skill of a Tris Speaker. A home-run hitter second only to Ruth, he excels as well in the special skills that were Cobb's—slashing the ball to the outfield, dropping bunts, getting on base and running infielders dizzy. Over the years he has been the man most likely on any given day to hit for the cycle, a man who in a single season has hit as many as fifty home runs and stolen as many as forty bases, in itself a rare parlay of talents. In more than a hundred years, baseball has not seen the likes of Willie, and when all the line drives, the bunts, the home runs and the stolen bases are totaled, all the head-first slides, all the cap-off catches in deepest center field, it seems impossible by any standard to bar Willie Mays from taking a place in baseball's all-time outfield.

If baseball often carries out the rags-to-riches

theme of Horatio Alger, and if in an earlier day the story began in a rural area with a white protagonist, today's version is notably changed. Today's Algeresque hero is likely to be black and often comes from the city streets, from the enclave if not the ghetto, and he is likely to bring with him the lean, hard look of deprivation, the grimness and resolve born of having had it tough, along with the impression that but for baseball he might have gone the other way.

When Frank Robinson was growing up in Oakland, the juvenile gangs were there, the organized as well as haphazard delinquency, but Robinson went in the opposite direction, not so much, one may guess, out of his love for good behavior as out of his love for baseball, and his refusal even then to be anything less than his own man. "I chose not to run with gangs because I was a loner," he writes. "I was a kid who always ran by himself."

Robinson today is still his own man, seasoned, leathery, lean as a whip, an exponent of hard-nosed, no-nonsense baseball. Today affluent, highly successful, he is as relentless in his will to win each game as he was earlier to crash the big time.

In 1955 he brought the pent-up anger of the kid with the occasional father to Cincinnati, and his anger crippled him at times but it also served him. In ten years with the Reds he performed brilliantly and often heedlessly—sometimes heedless of human sensibilities as well as of his own bodily safety. In six of his ten seasons with Cincinnati he led the league in getting hit by pitched balls. Few players showed more fervor in piling into second base to break up a double play, because this was one way to win a baseball game, this was hard-nosed, no-nonsense baseball. Today his legs and arms are laced with scars from spike wounds.

Robinson was traded to Baltimore before the 1966 season, and in the five years that followed, with Frank teaming up with another Robinson of note, Brooks, Baltimore won three pennants and two world championships. In Frank Robinson's first year with the Orioles he won the triple crown, and for this and other talents he was voted the American League's Most Valuable Player. Since he had already won the National League version of the same award when he was with the Reds, he is the only player in history to win the MVP award in both leagues.

Baseball has always been the core of his life, just as much now as in the early days in Oakland. To prolong his lifelong love affair with the game, he yearns to manage, and he brings outstanding qualifications. His anger has softened into maturity without diminishing the fierce desire to win. He is intelligent and a keen student of the game and all its many intricacies. It is quite possible that he may become the first black manager in major-league history. Meanwhile, he continues to give the game a high order of class and excellence, fielding his position flawlessly, breaking up double plays, throwing to the right base, coming up with the gut hit.

In the long history of World Series play, there have been many memorable performances. In 1931 there was the superb show put on by Pepper Martin, who batted .500 and ran wild on the bases, leading the Cardinals to victory over the mighty Philadelphia Athletics, Connie Mack's last great team. There was Babe Ruth's famous "called-shot" home run in the 1932 Series, in which the Yankees demolished the Cubs. In the fifth game of the 1956 Series, Don Larsen of the Yankees set down twenty-seven Brooklyn Dodgers in a row—the only perfect game in World Series history.

Whenever notable World Series feats are discussed in the years to come, it will be hard to overlook what Brooks Robinson of Little Rock, Arkansas, did to the Cincinnati Reds in the Series of 1970. With his bat he made a mighty contribution, whistling line drives past the ears of the Cincinnati pitchers, driving in runs in clutches, but it was the magic of his glove that will be long remembered. He played his position like the human vacuum cleaner he has been called, darting across the foul line to his right, lunging to his left, stealing sure base hits from the Reds' right-handed sluggers and in the end breaking their spirit. It was a performance seen and believed by a national television audience.

To Baltimore fans it was thrilling and perhaps a touch above the ordinary, yet not too far above the ordinary,because this was the sort of magic that Brooks had been performing ever since he came into the league in 1955. In the early years he was a light hitter, but he

kept working to make himself the complete ballplayer, and in 1962 there was Brooks, the nonpareil glove man, batting .303, and then in 1964 batting .317 and leading the league in runs-batted-in with 118. He confounded those who said he would never hit, just as he had confounded those who said years earlier that he would never make a major-league player. In Little Rock, where he lived an American-as-apple-pie boyhood, delivering newspapers and playing baseball, the verdict was that he was too slow for the big leagues. He may be slow but he is "quick"—with instant reflexes and sure hands—and his desire for self-improvement never ends. Even today, the acknowledged master of third-base play, he is among the first on the field for practice, and he still takes his twenty-five or thirty ground balls every day before the game. On most all-time, all-star teams, Pie Traynor fills the third-base slot. To those who watched Brooks Robinson in the second half of the 1950s and on through the 1960s, and perhaps particularly to those who watched what he did to the Reds in the 1970 World Series, it seemed highly doubtful that a greater third baseman ever lived.

It in no way belittles their enormous talents to say that Willie Mays and Frank and Brooks Robinson are among today's more colorful performers—Willie for his derring-do, Frank for his sometimes buccaneering approach to the game, Brooks for the excitement he engenders with his darting glove. One who is in their ultra-class as player and money-maker is Henry Aaron, the super-star of the Atlanta Braves, who made his way into the elite on sheer excellence.

Aaron, a native of Mobile, Alabama, left home at seventeen, taking his first train ride to join the Indianapolis Clowns, a noted barnstorming club. He had two dollars in his pocket, two pairs of pants and two sandwiches his mother had made him for the trip.

His entire major-league career has been spent with Milwaukee and with the Milwaukee club that became Atlanta. When he first came up as a rookie there was a brief public-relations campaign to make him colorful, to make him, as he describes it, "good copy." Aaron resisted. "I came to the Braves on business," he writes, "and I intended to see that business was good as long as I could."

Business has been very good, for a long, long time. Joining Milwaukee in 1954, in all the years since Aaron has merely been murdering the ball, year after year among the leaders in batting, home runs and runs-batted-in, year after year hanging up new hitting records. He got his first super-salary contract after the 1966 season.

Some players are reluctant to discuss their high salaries but Aaron is not among them. A press conference was held to announce the contract and a happy Hank Aaron was determined to show up looking the part of affluence, and determined that his wife should look the same.

"I wore my Sunday best," he related. "I had on a gray silk suit, one of those kind that shine back at you. Barbara had on a new mustard-colored coat I'd just bought her with a fur collar and fur cuffs. I'll just plain have to admit that getting into the $100,000 class gave me a feeling I had never had before."

The salary figures were announced. Flashbulbs popped. Henry Aaron and his shiny gray silk suit lit up the room. All in all, he concludes, it was "not bad for a kid who left home with two dollars in his pocket, two pairs of pants and two sandwiches in a paper bag."

Colorful has been defined as "abounding in startling contrasts; full of variety." In the case of a public performer, the elements of color may be many—a tainted private life for one, or a will to win so fierce that it approaches belligerence. Another is braggadocio, and yet another might be some departure from the physical norm—size, for example.

Mere size, of course, may do nothing more than qualify a man for a job in a circus sideshow or, as in the case of the unfortunate Primo Carnera, it may give him the sideshow appeal of a boxing freak. In no sport is size alone enough. Occasionally, however, physical size is combined with true skill, and the combination is crowd-pleasing. Frank Howard was born in Ohio, grew up to a very big boy indeed and now spends the off-season in Wisconsin, living on a yearly salary of approximately $500 per pound. During the season, the mammoth Howard lifts mammoth home runs out of the park for the Washington Senators, giving a mighty splash of color to a ball club that has been persistently drab over the years. Howard's physical proportions have done nothing to hurt his appeal at the gate.

Traditionally, baseball players have not been Gargantuan. The game requires no great size, and some of its greatest performers have been relatively small men. Eddie Collins, Frank Frisch, Rabbit Maranville and Nellie Fox come to mind. The great Willie Mays is himself only 5 feet 11 inches. Seldom, if ever, has there been a baseball player of the dimensions of Frank Howard, who looms 6 feet 7 inches and weighs usually in the neighborhood of 270. If Howard is colorful, it is his size that makes him so, for otherwise he is circumspect in the extreme, a modest, conservative man, crew-cut, bespectacled and abounding in the virtues and habits that tradition describes as all-American. But when all 6 feet 7 inches of him comes hulking up from the dugout, the very sight inspires excitement, and if he sometimes fields his position with the finesse that Carnera showed in the ring, all is forgiven when his huge bat speaks. It speaks with authority and often, booming out huge home runs that call for the tape measure, lending strength to the exciting, if dubious, premise that a Goliath can hit the ball farther than ordinary men and making each Howard turn at the bat an event. The crowd grows expectant. A giant is striding to the plate.

Harmon Killebrew, pride of the Minnesota Twins, is, like Frank Howard, a batsman of enormous power, and a fielder of questionable ability. Like Howard does now, Killebrew once wore the uniform of the Washington Senators, going to Minnesota with the team in 1961.

During the Civil War, so it is told, Harmon Killebrew's grandfather was heavyweight wrestling champion of the Union Army. Harmon himself has the build of a professional strong man—squat, powerful, with an enormous torso set upon a pair of short, thick legs. Muscles run in the family, and as a boy, away out west in Payette, Idaho, Harmon developed his muscles by lifting full milk cans and swinging baseball bats. By the time he was sixteen he was knocking baseballs lopsided. At seventeen he was playing semipro ball for Payette in the Idaho-Oregon Border League. He was spotted while playing for Payette by Herman Welker, who was then an Idaho senator. On Welker's next trip to Washington, he told his friend Clark Griffith, owner of the Washington Senators, that he had found a kid who could hit a baseball ten miles.

Griffith, a sagacious baseball man and always a bargain hunter, had until then resisted the bonus craze that afflicted so many major-league owners, but now he sent out a scout and Harmon Killebrew soon became Washington's first bonus player, signing for $30,000, a bargain. An even greater bargain—and another gift from Idaho semipro ball to the Washington Senators—was the incomparable Walter Johnson, who was spotted by a

Washington scout while pitching for Weiser, only fifteen miles from Payette, and who was signed for next to nothing.

Killebrew spent four seasons riding the bench or playing in the minors, but in 1959, installed as a regular, he began to terrorize American League pitching. During seventeen days in May of that year he hit two home runs in a game no less than five times. Still not twenty-three, he found himself judged the slugger most likely to break Babe Ruth's home-run record. In the year Roger Maris broke it, Harmon was an also-ran in the home-run race with forty-six, a typical Killebrew total. A streak hitter, who hits his home runs in clumps, he has gone along for years registering totals in the mid and high forties.

Affable, modest, now nearly bald, Killebrew carries the nickname "Killer," which suits his hitting but hardly his archetypal nice-guy personality. Although he may never break the single-season record, he has already hit enough home runs to qualify as one of the game's great right-handed sluggers.

Nearly half a century apart, two twenty-year-old outfielders wearing the uniform of the Detroit Tigers won the American League batting championship. The first was Ty Cobb, who in 1907 took the league batting title with an average of .350. Forty-eight years later, in 1955, Al Kaline collected two hundred hits and won the league crown with a mark of .340. Much was made of

the fact that Kaline thus became the youngest player in history ever to lead the league in hitting. The fact was that he was the youngest by a single day's grace—Cobb's birth date was December 18, Kaline's December 19.

Al Kaline was a schoolboy sensation, burning up the inter-high leagues around Baltimore with astronomical batting averages. Major-league scouts could hardly wait for him to graduate from high school so they could unload some of their bonus money. He was indeed signed the very day after his graduation for a bonus of $30,000, all of which he gave to his father. That was in 1953 and Kaline was eighteen.

As the 1954 season began, Kaline was installed as Detroit's regular right fielder. He was then less than a year out of high school, a fresh-faced blond kid who not only seemed to be a hitting natural but gave evidence of being one of the game's top defensive outfielders. That year, playing a complete season, he hit a very respectable .276 and once threw out three base runners in a single game.

In the following year when he ran his batting average up to a league-leading .340, there seemed no limit to what he might accomplish, for he was still only twenty, and his talents were enormous. He could hit, run and throw, and he patrolled the outfield with speed and grace. As an all-around ballplayer he was compared with Joe DiMaggio. He was even envisioned as a rival to Cobb in the annals of Detroit super-stars.

In 1971 Al Kaline began his nineteenth season in the

uniform of the Detroit Tigers. Day in, day out, year after year, he has given the Tigers a superior brand of offensive and defensive baseball. In Yankee Stadium he once broke his collarbone diving for a sinking liner. He made the catch and held on to the ball. When his career ends, his lifetime batting average will be right around .300. Kaline has left the mark of neither a Cobb nor a DiMaggio. Few players have. Instead, he has merely been excellent.

Admission into the super-salary class is often reserved for the big home-run hitter or the pitcher who consistently wins twenty games a year. Al Kaline is neither of these, nor is another member of the elite, Cincinnati's Pete Rose, an unquenchable outfielder. Rose has been called a throwback to the old days of hell-for-leather baseball, a man who would have been intensely admired by John McGraw or for that matter by any manager, because he plays the kind of baseball that preserves a manager's job.

A hometown boy, whose father played semipro football in Cincinnati, Pete was signed by the Reds at eighteen and sent to the minor leagues, where his all-out play earned him the nicknames "Hot Dog" and "Hollywood." The Reds brought him up in 1963 and stardom quickly followed.

Pete Rose is a super-hustler, who legs out a customary two hundred hits a season. Essentially a singles hitter, he lines the ball to the outfield or skids it through the infield, often stretching his singles into doubles and triples because he runs and hustles and never stops running and hustling. He hustles against fences in quest of fly balls. He skids on his nose trying for shoestring catches. After receiving a walk, he even runs at top speed to first base. Some players think there must be something wrong with him, doing all that unnecessary running and hustling—others say it makes them tired just to watch him. But his manager loves it and so do the fans who come to watch and so too do the moguls who pay him all that beautiful money. To major-league baseball he brings the enthusiasm of a sandlotter, the fervor of a Dink Stover going all out for Yale, the daring of a Pepper Martin. He is a modern player who might have been at home on the Baltimore Orioles of the 1890s, McGraw's team, or the St. Louis Cardinals Gashouse Gang of the 1930s, Pepper Martin's. Rose needs no special occasion, no critical series. On almost any given day he may be viewed tearing around the base paths and diving at a base headfirst—Pete Rose and a cloud of dust.

Carl Hubbell, one of history's premier southpaws, first looked over Juan Marichal when Juan was nineteen years old—he was amazed at what he saw. Expecting to find an unpolished rookie, he found instead that Marichal, at nineteen, was already pitching with the poise and expertise of a ten-year pro.

Marichal, the Dominican Republic's gift to the San

Francisco Giants, spent his boyhood on a farm, where he was often in the bad graces of his mother because he neglected his chores in favor of pitching a baseball. He threw a good curve at age ten and began experimenting with a screwball at fifteen. When he was eighteen he was "invited"—an invitation that bore the Trujillo imprimatur—to join the Dominican Air Force so that he could pitch for the Air Force baseball team. He pitched with success, although there was a notable day when the Air Force team lost a doubleheader, and for this Juan and his teammates were put in jail for five days and fined $2 each.

Marichal came up to the Giants in July 1960 and in his very first major-league start he pitched a one-hit shutout against the Phillies. Although his career has been marred by frequent injuries and by a near-riot precipitated when he banged catcher John Roseboro over the head with a bat, he has been one of the game's dominant figures for a decade, chalking up a twenty-games-plus record four years in a row and jumping into the blue-ribbon salary class after a 25-6 season in 1966.

In baseball history, Juan Marichal will be remembered as a pitching virtuoso with perhaps the most amazing array of pitches and deliveries the game has known. He uses a fast ball, a screwball and an assortment of curves and sliders, all of which he throws at varying speeds and with different deliveries. The result is understandably bewildering to National League batters, one of whom claims that Marichal's fast ball alone has ten different speeds. With it all he has precision control, and he also has doubtless the highest kick of any major-league pitcher. It has become his trademark and was adopted deliberately, he said, because as he swings his leg down it provides the leverage that beams his pitches low into the strike zone. A bad pitch, Marichal pointed out, is not a pitch that misses the plate, but one that gets too *much* of the plate, offering the batter a fat target. So he goes along nicking the strike zone, shaving corners, employing the pinpoint control that is so indispensable to pitching artistry. It is control that he learned not merely because he spent so much of his boyhood pitching baseballs, but because years ago, down on the farm, he perfected his ability to throw a ball exactly where he wanted it to go by spending long hours perfecting his aim with a slingshot. Marichal has always known what he wanted.

When Roberto Clemente was nineteen years old, playing a promising brand of baseball in and around his native Carolina, Puerto Rico, he received an offer of $10,000 to sign with the Brooklyn Dodgers. Jubilantly he accepted.

Very soon thereafter he got a jolt. The Milwaukee Braves were willing to top the Brooklyn offer and top it by plenty. The Milwaukee offer was $30,000.

Clemente's dilemma was quickly resolved by his mother. "You gave your word," she said sternly. "You keep your word."

Roberto kept his word and joined the Dodgers. He was sent to their top farm team, Montreal, for seasoning and, it was hoped, for hiding. The year was 1954 and the Dodgers had a splendid outfield of established stars. Unwilling to bring him up to the parent club, yet hoping to preserve him from the minor-league player draft, the Dodgers hoped he would not be noticed. It was a vain hope. After the 1954 season he was drafted by the Pittsburgh Pirates. Only a year away from his homeland and still speaking only his native Spanish, Roberto Clemente asked: "Donde está Pittsburgh?"

His first season with Pittsburgh was 1955 and he spent it lunging at the ball and, like so many young players, going for bad pitches. His overeagerness was a handicap and so too was a bad back. Indeed, Clemente over the years has suffered from a variety of ills that have kept him out of the game for long stretches—flu, nervous stomach, tension headaches and, most prominently, loose spinal discs, which have consistently given him back trouble.

Clemente's batting stroke was improved under the guidance of George Sisler, one of the game's all-time great batting stylists, who twice hit over .400. His back trouble was helped by enlistment with the U.S. Marines. To meet his service obligation to the United States, he did a six-month hitch with the Marines after the 1957 season, during which he had batted a mere .253. Hard work and a Spartan routine helped his back, he said, and beginning in 1958 his batting average started to climb. He won the National League batting championship in 1961, 1964 and 1965. Elevated to the super-salary class

after the 1966 season, he showed his appreciation by hitting .357 in 1967 to win the National League batting crown for the fourth time in seven years.

From the first, Clemente needed little help defensively. His arm is one of the best in baseball. He zings low trajectory bullets. He has thrown out as many as twenty base runners in a season and is credited with once having made a 420-foot throw from deep in the outfield to nip a runner at home plate.

The independently wealthy Tom Yawkey is one of baseball's most generous owners. He began spending big money after the 1934 season when he gave Washington a quarter of a million depression dollars for the services of Joe Cronin. Over the years he has continued to pour money into baseball, in salaries and in often lavish purchases, always hoping to be rewarded with pennant-winning teams, for along with his generosity Yawkey has the deep-rooted, enduring eagerness of a fan.

As a schoolboy athlete on Long Island, Carl Yastrzemski stirred up wide major-league interest. Scouts made their way to his door, offering big bonuses. Young Carl's business dealings were under the strict control of his father, who was holding out for top dollar. Top dollar proved to be in the neighborhood of $115,000, paid by Yawkey to make Yastrzemski a member of the Boston Red Sox.

Yaz joined Boston in 1961 and in his first six seasons

twice batted over .300, establishing himself as a good all-around performer, a good base runner and an excellent fielder with a strong arm.

In 1967 he paid off on Yawkey's investment, gladdening the hearts of Boston fans and especially the number-one fan, Tom Yawkey. The Red Sox had not won the pennant in twenty-one years, not since 1946, the year Ted Williams returned from World War II. In 1967 they figured to be far out of the money, but as the end of the season neared they were one of three teams very much in the running. Down the stretch Yaz carried the Red Sox, going wild at bat, heroic in the field, acting as team cheerleader and inspirational guide. On the final day of the season the Red Sox won the pennant by beating the Twins. Yaz that day went 4-for-4. For the season he won the triple crown.

The game that day was barely over when Yastrzemski was boosted into the big-money class for the second time, the first having been his bonus. All those years Tom Yawkey had waited for another pennant and for another Ted Williams or a reasonable facsimile. Now he was carried away. "Carl is a better fielder than Ted," he said, "and I think Carl may even be a better all-around player than Ted was." Suffused with gratitude, Yawkey said he wanted to do something special for Yastrzemski. So that very day he raised his salary approximately $50,000.

In the World Series Yaz, with a mighty assist from pitcher Jim Lonborg, made it all look very good. He might even have taken the Sox all the way to the world championship except that he and the Red Sox happened to run into Bob Gibson who, with the Series tied at three games apiece, won the deciding game on a three-hitter.

For Bob Gibson, who began life in a four-room shack in an Omaha slum, the World Series has been a special showcase. In 1964, against the Yankees, he pitched twenty-seven innings, winning two games, losing one and setting a strikeout record of thirty-one for the Series. In 1968, pitching against Detroit, he won the first game on a 4–0 shutout, setting a single-game Series record for strikeouts with seventeen.

Bob Gibson has been a superlative pitcher for the St. Louis Cardinals for a decade. In 1970 he won the National League Cy Young Award for the second time in three years. Among other accomplishments, he has logged twenty or more victories five times, eclipsing a Cardinals' club record he had shared with the great Dizzy Dean.

The 1967 World Series with Yastrzemski and the Red Sox had been over about a month when Gibson and his wife received an invitation with an illustrious seal. They were being invited to have dinner at the White House, as the guests of President and Mrs. Johnson.

Gibson has written of his life in a book aptly entitled *From Ghetto to Glory.* He never knew his father, never even saw a picture of him. He died three months before Gibson was born, leaving Bob's mother with seven kids to rear on the wages of a laundress.

Bob Gibson and his wife accepted the invitation and went to the White House. They were quickly spotted by Vice President Hubert Humphrey, an ardent sports fan, who congratulated Gibson for what he had just done to the Red Sox. What he had done was pitch and win three complete ball games, giving up a total of three runs and fourteen hits. The fourteen-hit total tied a Series record that went deep into time, set in the 1905 Series by the masterful Christy Mathewson. For this and other feats, Bob would go on to a salary of something in the area of $135,000.

At the White House, while waiting for dinner to be announced, Vice President Humphrey and Bob Gibson continued to discuss baseball. The Vice President happened to notice that he and Gibson were the only men present who were wearing blue shirts with their dinner jackets. Jokingly, Humphrey said this had to prove that he and Gibson were the only guys there with any class. Bob Gibson and the Vice President laughed together.

"How do you measure poverty?" Gibson asks in his book. "I wore the same coat for three or four years. It was a hand-me-down from one of my brothers and I wore it until it had too many holes in it. I had one pair of shoes and I wore them until they practically fell off my feet. When they got holes in the bottom, I put a piece of cardboard in them.

"Christmas was something special. One Christmas I got a truck. It was a red truck and it had only three wheels and I couldn't understand why one wheel was missing. But I loved that little red truck with three wheels more than anything else in the world."

Presently, when the announcement came, Bob Gibson offered his arm, and he and his wife walked into the state dining room for dinner at the White House.

Baseball, a national phenomenon, is like that. It has a way of opening doors.

The salaried elite

by LeRoy Neiman

LeRoy Neiman is a painter best known for his sports portrayals.
He has painted for *Playboy* magazine since that publication's
inception, creating the feature "Man at His Leisure." He was
instructor of drawing at the School of the Art Institute of Chicago
for ten years and instructor of painting with the Atlanta Poverty
Program for two years. His oil paintings have been included in
major exhibitions such as the Carnegie International in Pittsburgh,
the Corcoran American Exhibition in Washington, D.C.
and the American Exhibition of Oil Painting in Chicago. His
one-man shows, twenty in number and all successful, include
four at the Hammer Galleries in New York, his exclusive
representative in that city, as well as others in London, Paris and
Florence. He is represented in permanent collections of the
Minneapolis Institute of Art, Wodham College, Oxford, England,
the National Museum of Sport in Art, New York,
and in numerous private collections.

In his paintings, Mr. Neiman splashes vibrant paint across
canvas with a boldness and flair reflective of the intensity,
strength and immediacy of his subjects. His kaleidoscopic
colors—swirling pinks, yellows, reds—emotively arrive at a
straightforward and honest realism.

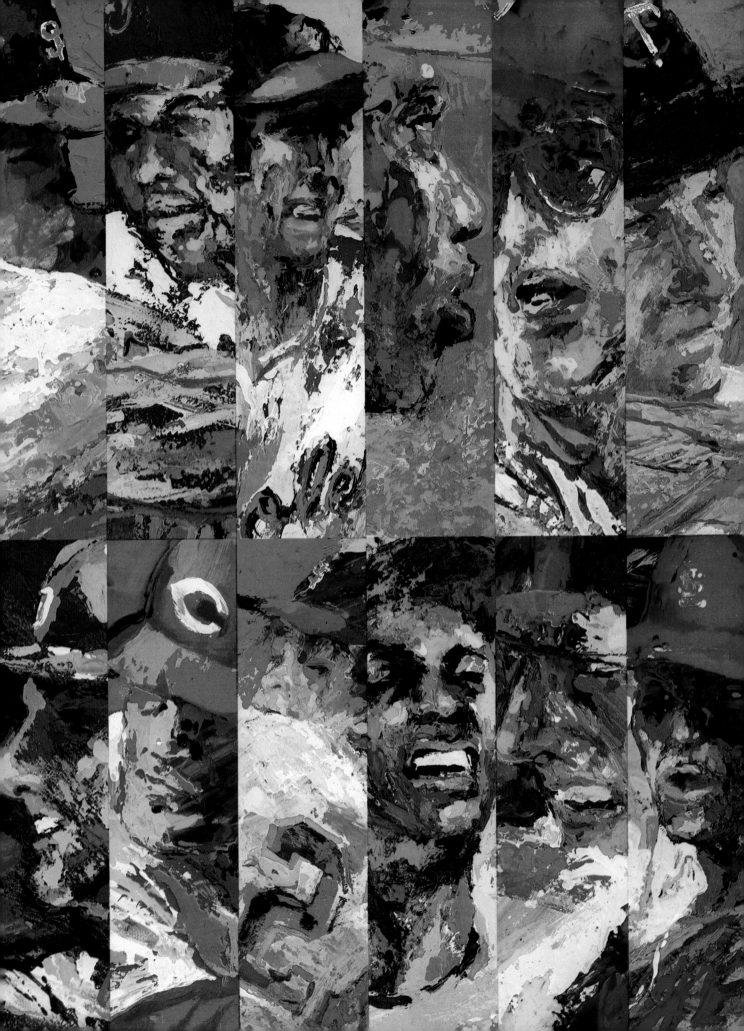

Willie Mays

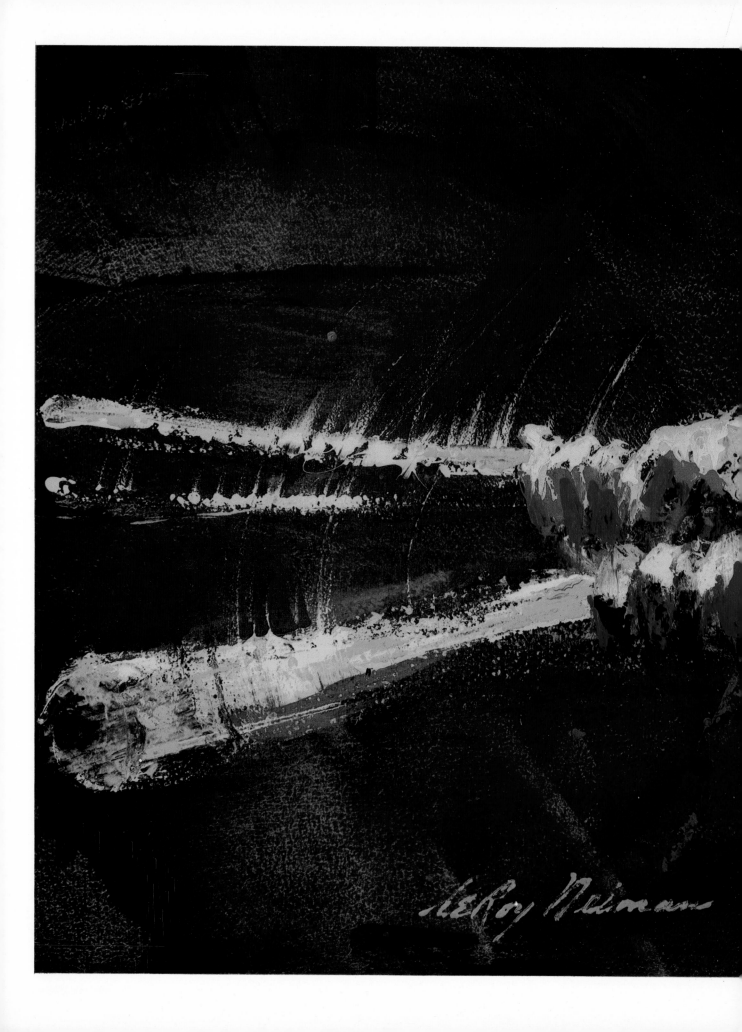

Frank Robinson

LeRoy Neiman

Brooks Robinson

Hank Aaron

Frank Howard

Harmon Killebrew

Al Kaline

Pete Rose

Juan Marichal

Roberto Clemente

Carl Yastrzemski

LeRoy Neiman

Bob Gibson

The man in blue

umpiring

by Al Barlick with Jim Enright

There are two well-known groups of "men in blue"—policemen and umpires. Both have complete authority when performing their duties. Both are respected and cursed. Both are made up of proud men. There comparison ceases.

The policemen can expect reward upon completion of a job well done—perhaps decoration, applause or a simple "thank you." An umpire receives none of these. Only his errors (or what fans decide are errors) bring him attention. He is booed, never cheered. What the psychological makeup of such a man must be and what the job truly entails are questions to which Al Barlick addresses himself in these pages.

Al Barlick is a veteran of thirty years' umpiring service in the National League. He has worked seven World Series and six All-Star games. Al Barlick is considered not only the most outspoken of his profession, but the best.

Jim Enright is a sports writer for *Chicago Today*. He is also a veteran basketball referee for the Big Eight, Big Ten, Missouri Valley, National Basketball League and National Basketball Association. He is the author of "*Mr. Cub*," the newly published story of Ernie Banks.

During the 1970 World Series I heard something that made me mad. I was listening to the Orioles and the Reds battle it out on a portable radio in the backyard while I wrestled with some shrubs I was transplanting.

Chuck Thompson, one of the radio announcers, said: "There is a National League umpire officiating behind the plate today. That means there will be lots of low pitches called strikes. This is one of the differences between the American League and the National League umpires. In the American League, they call a lot of high pitches strikes."

What malarkey!

A strike is a strike and a ball is a ball. There is just one strike zone, from the top of the knee to the top of the letters, and it's the same in both leagues.

There are, as a matter of fact, almost as many misconceptions about umpires and umpiring as there are major-league ballplayers.

I'll never forget my first major-league game behind the plate. I'd been up from the International League less than a week on a look when I was assigned to work the dish in a game between the Cincinnati Reds and the Phillies. Johnny Vander Meer was pitching for the Reds against the Phillies' Hugh Mulcahy.

During one of the early innings Bennie Warren, catching for the Phillies, really let me have it after a ball call. Warren's jawing became progressively bitter until Mulcahy stepped off the mound and yelled to his catcher: "Leave him alone, the ball was low."

There wasn't another peep out of Warren for the rest of the game. The Reds won, 4–3, in thirteen innings to clinch the 1940 National League pennant.

Definitive out call.

In the next thirty years, no one ever defended one of my ball and strike calls in the Mulcahy manner.

Frequently the easiest man for an umpire to win an argument from is the manager. Some of them neglect to read up on the rule book until they become involved in a rhubarb with one of the gentlemen officiating a game and then it's too late.

Once I bounced a manager after he admitted that I'd made the right call. He was Leo Durocher (managing the Dodgers) and it was his first chase after sitting out his year's suspension.

The Dodgers were playing the

Pirates early in the season in Pittsburgh and the score was tied going into the bottom of the eighth. The Pirates loaded the bases and big Tiny Bonham was the runner on third. Harry Taylor went into his windup, stopped and then started another windup.

I called a balk, which allowed Bonham to score and the other two runners to each advance a base.

Durocher charged out, yelling, "I know it was a balk but you are a . . ." Needless to say, he used a forceful Anglo-Saxon term that gets people thrown out of ball games.

As soon as he said it, I chased him. He continued to call me just about every name in the book. I told him I couldn't stop him from talking but I sure as hell could make him pay for what he was saying. That didn't seem to faze Leo. He had a few more epithets he wanted to use up.

Finally he left and we finished the game. The next day was Saturday and my turn to work the plate. As I dressed for the game with my partners, George Barr and Lee Ballanfant, I had a bad feeling.

Pee Wee Reese met us at home plate with the Dodgers' batting-order card and left quickly after we checked it out. Often the two managers or the two team captains will stick around and jaw for a while after all the official business is transacted.

We talk about almost anything in those huddles: an unusual play in yesterday's game or some fielding feat we'd read about in the morning papers or anything else that pops into anybody's mind. After all, you can check the lineups and review the ground rules in a fast minute or two and it's boring after that just standing around waiting for game time.

With no one to talk to, I decided

to get busy and dust off home plate. While I'm leaning over with my broom, I hear those dulcet tones that can only be my "pal" Durocher. He's yelling, "It's all right, we haven't begun the game yet."

I straighten up and tell him, "Mr. Manager, if you want to see this game, you'd better shut your mouth."

He hollers back, "I won't shut up until I get good and ready."

How about that? My partners hadn't yet reached their positions and I'm chasing Leo again. He storms out to the plate, repeating everything he'd thought to say the night before—and more. Eventually he leaves again.

Think that one out. First, last night, by his own admission, I'd made the right call. Result: I had to bounce him twice, in the eighth inning of the Friday game and again on Saturday before a ball was thrown.

I've had my share of run-ins with players, managers, even—on occasion—with league head-quarters. Almost all of them have been momentary flare-ups. A flash of anger and it's gone and forgotten. Just about the only on-and-off, running feud worth recording concerns that model of placidity I've just been talking about, Leo Durocher.

I got off to an early start with

Manager Bill Rigney and Bob Rodgers sandwich umpire Larry Napp in another case of "try to see it my way."

Leo. In fact, had I given Leo a real opportunity, I think he would have liked to run me right out of the majors my first full season in 1942.

It seemed as if we were always locking horns over something or other. Usually during these heated discussions Leo would get around to "firing" me. Finally one day I told him, "Leo, if you really can get me fired, that's OK with me because then the job isn't worth having." He didn't much care for those words, but that didn't slow him up one bit.

One night in St. Louis in a game between the Dodgers and the Cardinals, a ball was hit to left and there was a question whether Pete Reiser had caught or trapped the ball. I called it a trap, Reiser charged me, saying, "Al, I caught that ball."

Trying to be as diplomatic as possible, I told Pete I didn't think he did and that was why I'd called it a trap. Reiser tells me what he thinks of my call. It's as good a name as Leo might have used and it's a no-no on the baseball field. Pete's gone. Now comes Durocher, and what a time he gives me! He's kicking dirt at me, so I walk from the skinned part of the infield to the outfield grass.

Leo is still kicking. His spikes or whatever he was wearing skid in the grass and his foot hits the back of my heel. Now I'm boiling. I tell him that one of us isn't going to be here at the game tomorrow night, meaning I'm reporting him to the league president and recommending suspension.

Leo counters with a remark that still bothers me: "That's all right, I know what's going on."

Ford Frick, who was then the league president and my boss, wasn't in the office when I called New York with my report the following morning. I told the

assistant who took my call that I was going home if Durocher wasn't suspended.

Apparently the league offices reached Frick with my message. He immediately fined as well as suspended Leo—and I didn't have to go home. Before mailing in my report—customary after a telephone report—I penned a postscript asking Frick to call Durocher to his office the next time I was in New York to have him explain what he meant when he'd said, "I know what's going on."

Later on, when I was in New York, I asked Frick what had happened. He didn't tell me. He said, "The hell with it. Any time Durocher gives you trouble, chase him."

Speaking of misconceptions, one of the oldest claims in baseball says that an umpire evens up a bad call.

That's plain silly, completely incorrect and improper. When an umpire misses a call, he knows it. Nobody has to tell him. He simply bears down extra hard to make certain he doesn't miss another. Let me tell you something. When you are out there day after day for a full season, it's not difficult to blow one.

I've known times when I've seen a pitch come right down the middle and I've called it a ball. Why? I can't tell you. You just do it. But there's no such thing as another call to even things up. Never. No way.

Since the introduction of the instant replay on television, I've said, and I mean it: If the camera shows that the umpire has made a wrong call, find a way to change it right there on the spot.

Instant replay or no, we're right such a good percentage of the time I'm willing to pay anybody $500 for every wrong call I make if he'll give me $5 for every one I call that's right.

I remember one I missed. It was in Cincinnati when the Cubs were playing the Reds. Attempting to sacrifice, a Cubs' batter bunted a

ball that hit the plate and bounced foul.

Babe Pinelli, who was working the plate, doesn't make a signal and looks at me. I think he wants help on the play. Just as I signal foul—I saw the ball six to eight inches foul—Babe pumps the fair signal. So the Reds miss getting the double play. Bill McKechnie, their manager, comes out of the dugout.

"What the hell is going on?"

Bill and Babe talk a while and then start toward me. I tell them right off that I've goofed. It was Babe's call and I had no right to make one until the ball reached or passed a base.

We talk some more and finally McKechnie says, "What am I supposed to do now?"

I say, "Bill, as far as I'm concerned, you have me dead all the way."

McKechnie paws the dirt with his foot for a few seconds and finally leaves, giving me an "Oh, hell" look of pure disgust.

That's one of the differences between managers. Some can accept a wrong call, others can't. McKechnie knew I was wrong but he didn't try to make a big deal out of it. I respect him for that.

I've been the plate umpire for just one no-hit, no-run game. Ewell Blackwell pitched it for the Reds against the Boston Braves in Cincinnati, June 18, 1947. The Reds took the game, 6–0.

You've heard about the super-stition that teammates never talk about a no-hitter while their pitcher is in the act of pitching one. The umpires are in easy view of the scoreboard and we know what is going on. We also appreciate the

Tony Venzon gets across the point that Bernie Carbo has been tagged out by Mark Belanger. Davey Johnson backs up the play.

significance and it's only human nature for the umpires to bear down a bit harder when a no-hitter reaches the eighth or ninth inning.

Twice in one season I saw Jim Maloney of the Reds go ten innings without giving up a hit, but I wasn't behind the plate. Jim lost the first one to the Mets on two hits in the eleventh, but he beat the Cubs in Chicago and won the second game.

During a day-in day-out, year-to-year association with managers and players, an umpire can make up his own catalog of them, plus or minus. An umpire can—but he doesn't. You wipe the slate clean with the start of each new game. There simply isn't room for grudges.

Umpires take as much pride in their performance as any player does. Usually no one stops to ask how an ump feels when he boots a call. I'll tell you: lousy.

This was painfully true for me after a weird episode in a game at Wrigley Field between the Cardinals and the Cubs.

Stan Musial was the batter for the Cardinals. The count was three and two and Bob Anderson's next pitch was high and inside. Sammy Taylor, the Cubs' catcher, sees the ball roll to the backstop. He makes no attempt to retrieve it, apparently thinking it was a foul tip.

Vic Delmore, the umpire behind the plate, signals ball four and Anderson and Taylor begin to argue the call. Two things happen then: Musial jogs off to first and Taylor asks umpire Delmore for a new ball. Vic gives it to him and Taylor promptly flips it out to Anderson.

I'm working at first base and I see Alvin Dark, the Cubs' third baseman, running hard toward the plate. I figure he's going to charge Delmore and I run in to help Vic. Instead, Dark runs right past the plate and goes to the backstop. He returns quickly with the original ball. Meanwhile, the Cards on the bench behind first are yelling to Musial to take second.

Now comes something I never want to see happen again. Dark and Anderson both throw out to second base. Dark's throw is low and is fielded by Ernie Banks, then playing shortstop for the Cubs. Anderson's throw is high and sails over the head of Tony Taylor, the Cubs'

Harry Wendelstedt takes a breather.

second baseman. Musial slides into second. When he gets up and starts for third, Banks tags him out with the ball Dark had thrown to him. The umpire makes the out call.

Solly Hemus, the St. Louis manager, of course protests immediately, because there were two baseballs in play simultaneously. The Cubs argue that Musial is out because he was tagged with the original ball in play. We agree.

Nothing comes of the protest because the Cards win the game, 4–1. We actually don't learn all the details of the play until some time later. It seems that Pat Peiper, the Cubs' public address system

announcer, on the field as authorized personnel, had tossed the baseball to Dark when he had yelled, "Give me the ball."

Right there it was interference, pure and simple, and the ball was dead. Musial should have stayed on first, safe, instead of being out at second.

All the umpires, Bill Jackowski and Shag Crawford as well as Vic and myself, felt bad about the play. We'd called it as we saw it—wrong.

Two apparently is meant to be my unlucky number. I was once involved in a two-out inning—and when is the last time you ever heard of that?

This time the Giants were playing the Dodgers in Brooklyn, and I was working with Pinelli. Dolf Camilli singled with one out. Joe Medwick followed with a blue darter bing-bing directly at Billy Rigney, the Giants' shortstop.

Rigney fielded the ball, and threw to Mickey Witek for the force of Camilli at second. Witek straddles the base, but hasn't touched it. I signal Camilli safe, but call Medwick out on Witek's throw to first.

Camilli gets up, dusts himself off and trots off the field. So do all the Giants, thinking they have completed an inning-ending double play.

As the Dodgers take the field, Pee Wee Reese stops and asks me: "Al, didn't you signal Camilli safe at second?"

I kept right on walking toward my position in back of first base and never answered Pee Wee. It's the coaches' job to instruct the runners whether they are out or safe. The umpires can't because that would be helping one team to the detriment of the other. Reese didn't press the issue, and it wasn't mentioned again until I reached our dressing room with Pinelli.

As we dressed, Babe said: "Your best call of the day was not answering Reese. You proved silence is still the best policy."

I've done a lot of thinking about that particular play. While I still think Reese was guessing when he asked me about the safe call on Camilli, there could have been a lot of repercussions. Say the Dodgers had had a runner on third at the time, and he scored while the Giants were making what they thought was a double play.

A legally scored run can never be taken away from a team, and what do you think might have happened while I was trying to explain that one? I've got to think that some of those rabid Dodgers' fans would have hurried out and found a scaffold and hung Ol' Albert then and there at second base.

Respect is the common denominator between the manager and the umpire. The manager respects you for your ability to make the right call, and you respect him for his ability to accept it. There are a lot of gentlemen managers, men like Walter Alston, Preston Gomez, Red Schoendienst and Gil Hodges, as well as former-day leaders, such as McKechnie, Billy Southworth, Burt Shotton, Mel Ott, Charley Grimm, Eddie Sawyer and Casey Stengel.

After all the many episodes I have been involved in with Leo Durocher, I think Leo has respect for me if he has respect for anybody. In every dispute Manager Durocher always knew just how far he could go with Umpire Barlick before something happened—like me chasing him.

They call Gene Mauch, the Montreal manager, a fiery little guy. He is, every inch of him. But there is something about Mauch that separates him from most of the holler guys. It's this: Mauch reads and studies the rule book. When he comes out to ask about a rule, you had better have the right answer for him or you're in trouble. I can't blame him. If an umpire lacks a positive knowledge of any rule, he just doesn't belong in the major leagues.

I admire Mauch. He never presses a situation after the right rule has been applied. I can't say this about all managers.

A game between the old Boston Braves and the Cardinals in Sportsman's Park in St. Louis is a case in point. The Braves loaded the bases, and Max West was the hitter. The runner at third took a long lead, as if he was going to break for the plate. Lon Warneke, the Cardinals' pitcher, sensed this, stepped off the rubber and threw to the plate. West swung and hit the ball off the right-field screen for a double.

I was working the plate and called West's hit void because he had hit an illegal pitch. When Warneke had backed off the mound, he had become an infielder instead of a pitcher and his throw wasn't a legal pitch.

Mr. Stengel, the Braves' manager, paid me a quick visit and complained: "My man West hit a double and I haven't got anything on the scoreboard to show for it. I want my runs."

I explained the illegal pitch. Casey stalked back to the Braves' bench, muttering: "Oh hell, everything else has happened to me and now this— an illegal pitch. I never heard of such a thing before, but that's what I get for becoming a manager instead of a lawyer."

An umpire isn't a lawyer—at least I never heard of one acting in both capacities—but, nevertheless, his job is a full-time application of the rules hitched to good judgment. Frequently umpires are invited to clinics to share their techniques with younger men.

Whenever I'm working the plate, I like to drift after the ball is hit. This helps two ways: It assures the umpire of staying out of the way of the runner as well as the catcher, and leaves him in good position to call the play.

Throws to the plate, especially those from the outfield, all act differently. Some skip. Some bounce. Some veer out of the catcher's or the backup man's reach. By drifting, the umpire is always in position to make a call.

In a catcher's pursuit of a foul ball, the first thing to remember is: stay out of his way to avoid a collision.

With four-man crews in the National League, the umpire at second base works inside on the infield. In this manner he sees all the action: the scoop-up of the ball, the throw, the catch, the pivot and the throw to first if there is one. Every movement is made in full view of the umpire working inside.

Working behind the base, an umpire can be screened out of the play, unable to make a correct call. This is especially true if an infielder drops the ball when throwing to first after completing a force-out at second.

Some umpires have a tendency to call a play too soon. Others anticipate it. I say this is bad officiating. Adoption of the magic rule *wait!* will spare embarrassment. *Wait* until the play is completed— then call it decisively. I have seen times when Jocko Conlan had a runner called out before he was halfway to first.

Some umpires, like some players, simply aren't ready when they come to the major leagues. Years ago the Chicago Cubs brought up a shortstop named Roy Smalley. He was a real whiz kid, seemingly able to do it all.

Smalley looked like an immediate star. Then something happened. He never did improve. Why? In my book, because he was rushed along too fast.

World Series incident. Umpire Ken Burkhart misses missed tag at plate by Ellie Hendricks, but makes the only call he can—out. Bernie Carbo argues violently, but had Burkhart not interfered, out would have been made easily.

118

As for umpires, there was never a more nervous and highly strung young man than Eddy Vargo when he arrived in the majors. They were about to send Vargo back when I asked that he be assigned to my crew. I welcomed the opportunity to work with Eddy, and I don't mind saying he developed into an outstanding umpire. He's very good right now, but he's going to become a great one in time. Eddy still hasn't reached his peak.

Anytime there is my kind of discussion, this question is posed: Why do so few players become umpires? Offhand, I can think of these players who did: George Moriarty, Jocko Conlan, Babe Pinelli, Ed Rommel, Charlie Berry, Ken Burkhart, Tom Gorman, Frank Secory and Lon Warneke.

I always have felt that Warneke, a great pitcher during his playing days, was rushed to the majors too rapidly as an umpire. Lon was promoted by Ford Frick after just two years in the Pacific Coast League.

120

One night before expansion, Lon worked at the Polo Grounds in New York and I was in Brooklyn. We met later, and Lon said: "I just worked a perfect game for thirteen innings. I was the plate umpire and didn't miss a pitch."

I know Lon wasn't kidding, but I had to tell him his "perfect" game had to be the first ever. I never umpired a perfect game and don't know of any umpire who has. Great pitcher that he was, Lon drew the most heat as an umpire when calling balls and strikes behind the dish.

There is a certain dedication that players seem to lack when they switch to umpiring. That is the only way I can explain why only a few former players stick it out and get to the majors as umpires.

There are exceptions. One of them is Babe Pinelli. Babe played eight years in the majors, six with the Reds, and then became an outstanding umpire. He never

From left: Obvious out call is made as Hal Lanier forces Cleon Jones; Washington's Ed Stroud doesn't think his call was as obvious; Al Barlick examines a bat claimed to be oversized.

Even an umpire can flinch at times.

Tony Venzon calls the Series.

Sparky Anderson "concedes" to Burkhart.

122

missed a game, not even a single inning, in twenty-one years as a man in blue.

George Moriarty is another. He played more than a thousand games during a thirteen-year major-league career before becoming manager of the Detroit Tigers in 1927 and 1928. In between playing and managing, George became a major-league umpire and worked two World Series. After his two years of managing, he went back to umpiring and worked three more World Series.

Bill Stewart used to umpire in the National League during the baseball season and then switch to coaching the Chicago Black Hawks of the National Hockey League during the winter. This two-hatting is tough to do now that the seasons in spectator sports overlap.

I had a different kind of job after the 1947 baseball season. When I got back home that fall I was offered a job as a miner at Capitol Mine Peabody No. 57. It was good pay and not too far from home. The trouble was, the workers called a

strike, which was followed by layoffs. I didn't get too much work after all that winter, but it was enough to help the family out with its budget and it helped me stay in good physical shape.

Before the close of the 1948 season, during my last trip to New York, I stopped by the league office to say good-bye to Frick. We talked a while and then he asked me what I planned to do that winter. I told him I was open to any reasonable offer. Why?

"I hope you aren't planning on returning to the coal mine," he told me. That was the first time I realized he had known what work I had done the previous winter. I wasn't ashamed of the job, just surprised that he knew.

I told him I couldn't afford to sit around all winter without any income. He said, "Working in the mine you are running the risk of an injury. What if something happened to your eyes? It would jeopardize your career as an umpire. That's why I'm hoping you can find a different kind of job."

Sure, true enough, but what job? If I had been a player in that situation, chances are somebody would have come up with something specific.

It's different with an umpire. Nobody worries about you once the season's over. They may not want

you to do something that would risk your not coming back next year, but they don't really do anything about it.

To tell the truth, umpires don't move up baseball's financial ladder too rapidly. Some of us think that's wrong. We're an integral part of the game of baseball. Yet we work in isolation, sort of a temporary attachment that's removed once the season ends. All of this had considerable to do with what happened on the first day of the 1970 championship series.

I'm talking about the umpires' one-day strike. I really don't like what we did. I owe a lot to baseball, but I claim that the umpires were forced to take action. Since the strike, some people have asked why I was on the picket line. I was there to help better the conditions for the people in my profession. My being on the picket line represented my personal feelings.

I'm nearing the fifty-five-year retirement age and the chances are I won't be umpiring another World Series or All-Star game, but this doesn't lessen my desire to see baseball reckon fairly with the

Emmett Ashford vs. Boog Powell.

Point indicates ball is in play.

Davis and Gilliam lose to Dezelan.

men in blue. They are doing a very important job and they want to be properly recognized. I don't see that this is asking too much.

Frankly, I was flattered when the National League umpires in their first move to organize had Augie Donatelli call me to say that the boys had decided to form their own association but felt they'd be dead if I didn't go along. I told Augie, "Let's get started." The eventual vote of the men was seventeen to three in favor. The association's unity has been outstanding in helping better the umpire's life. We've had salary increases, bigger and better numbers for our pension plan and have won added fringe benefits. All I'm trying to say is that umpires are part of baseball and deserve equal treatment.

Enough of that. Let's talk about 1954, the year the New York Giants swept the Cleveland Indians in the World Series, snapping a string of seven straight victories in the classic for the American League. I have my reasons for

remembering 1954. That was the year—and the only time—I was involved in a protest that was upheld.

It was a late September game between the Reds and the Braves in Milwaukee. The Braves led 3-1 with Cincinnati batting in the ninth. Gus Bell was on second and Wally Post was on first, with one out.

Bob Borkowski fanned on a wild pitch by Warren Spahn. Del Crandall, the Braves' catcher, ran down the ball and threw to Eddie Mathews, trying to retire Bell at third. When this failed, Mathews threw to first. His throw hit Borkowski and rolled into right field, letting both Bell and Post score with the tying runs.

The umpires held a conference and the four of us decided that the game was over because Borkowski's illegal presence on the base paths had drawn the throw. On this theory we called Bell and Borkowski both out and ruled that Milwaukee had won, 3-1.

The Reds protested and Warren Giles, then the National League president, ruled that the umpires under game pressure had called it correctly according to their interpretation. However, Giles said, he couldn't accept this with a "clear conscience," and thereby ordered the game resume at the point of the protest.

This set up a most unusual situation: three major-league clubs in the same park at the same time. The Reds had to return to Milwaukee to finish out the protested game before the St. Louis Cardinals met the Braves for the day's regularly scheduled game.

In the protested game finish, Johnny Temple hit a first-pitch single to score Bell and Post, making it 3–3. When the Braves batted in their half of the ninth, George Metkovich singled home the run the Braves needed for a win. (The Braves won the regular game too, 4-2.)

I'll never forget that protest. The league president said that we (the umpires) were right and then had to rule against us.

Next, the loaded pitch. Every major-league umpire knows one when he sees it and we know the pitchers who violate the rule. We get bulletins to look for such pitches and we bounce violators after a warning. We also get bulletins not to put our hands on a pitcher when we suspect he's loading it up. Instead, we are told to ask the pitcher to hand us his glove or his cap if we want to make an inspection.

123

But that isn't the way to stop this maneuver. The general managers can stop it in a hurry if they put some teeth into the rule. I'm not talking about a fine. That isn't going to stop anything, because most clubs pay the fines anyway. I'm talking about suspension. When a pitcher is caught, suspend him five days the first time and from fifteen to twenty days for his second offense. That will stop the loaded pitch in a hurry. There isn't a ball club that can afford the loss of a pitcher for such an extended period of time. Until then, nothing much is going to happen to stop the use of that kind of pitch.

Some people think an umpire is so engrossed in umpiring that he never finds any humor in the game. Wrong again. For example, when I went on a post-season tour of Japan with the Cardinals, Curt Flood got off one of his deadpan quips and I still laugh when I think about it.

They were interviewing Curt on a sports program to be fed back to the United States on radio. He was asked about the difference in the strike zone between the States and Japan. Flood said: "I've always been taught the strike zone was from the top of the knee to the top of the letters, but I had to come to Japan to learn they meant the top of the letters on my cap." Curt's line broke up the show.

During that same trip, Bob Gibson was having a rougher time than usual. One day on the bus back to the hotel after the game, Gibson, still upset, said to me, "If I ever beef again at a ball or strike call by an American umpire, tell him to run me right out of the park."

I promised Bob that his message would be relayed to all the National League men. Last summer during a game at St. Louis, Gibson and umpire Dick Stello were exchanging a few differences of opinion about balls and strikes.

The static became pretty heated and Gibson glared over at me. Before he could say anything, I yelled: "Maybe you'd like me to put in a call for one of those fine Japanese umpires and have him delivered gift-wrapped directly to you."

Gibson managed a faint smile— something you don't see much from him in the heat of battle—and never said another word to Stello.

Every umpire has a story to tell about how he got started. I'm no exception. As kids from poor families, we played baseball with a broomstick and a kernel of corn. Match that. Also, our pitcher was the umpire as well. If the batter failed to swing at a pitch, the umpire-pitcher had to call it a ball or a strike. That's where I developed my gusty gravelly S-T-R-I-K-E call.

I was one of the umpires in the longest nine-inning game in baseball history: four hours and eighteen minutes. It was an October day in 1962 in Los Angeles and the Dodgers beat the Giants, 8–7, in the second game of a pennant play-off. Both teams used a record number of players—forty-two in all.

Speaking of records, I would like to know if something in the 1946 World Series isn't a first. Each of the four umpires was paid $2,500 to work. The Series involved the Cardinals and the Boston Red Sox. Because both teams played in small parks—Sportsman's in St. Louis and Fenway in Boston—the

shares for the losers (Red Sox) were $2,140.89 each, $359.11 less than the fee paid each umpire.

Umpires aren't supposed to have heroes, but I have one nevertheless. My hero is Bill Klem, also my candidate to be the first National League umpire admitted to the Hall of Fame. (The American League already has one—Tommy Connolly.)

I broke into the majors working with Klem and he had more to do with my progress than anybody else. I literally loved this gentleman, who relished being called Mr. Arbitrator. It was during a spring-training period that I had my last visit with Bill at his home in Florida.

He had retired but baseball remained his life. As I was leaving, he said: "Albert, I want to tell you something. You are going to meet a lot of umpires during your career. Some you will like, some you won't. Some will be culls. Others will be foul balls. Regardless, I want you to help them. You can and you will help them. When you are helping them, you are helping baseball."

The great plays

by Joseph Reichler

Unlike most other sports, whose games in their entirety are remembered as being great, baseball greatness is most often recalled for its individual plays.

Joseph Reichler has chosen nineteen plays he holds as being uniquely memorable. On the basis of pure numbers, the selections here are necessarily arbitrary, but with three exceptions each play had a crucial bearing on a pennant race or on a World Series outcome. Those three exceptions are given a place on the sheer wonder of their ever having occurred.

Mr. Reichler is the author of many baseball and sports books and articles. He has been accused of knowing more baseball history off the top of his head than most people can find in a book. At present he is Director of Public Relations in the office of the Commissioner of Baseball.

How Frank Baker Became Home Run Baker

126

Frank Baker, famous third baseman of the Philadelphia Athletics' glory years of 1910–14, hit exactly nine home runs in 1911. Yet before that year had come to an end he was known the country over as Home Run Baker, a sobriquet he was to carry to his final resting place. Why? Here's why.

It all began in the second game of the 1911 World Series between Connie Mack's Athletics and John J. McGraw's New York Giants. The first game, played two days earlier, had been won by the Giants, 2–1. Christy Mathewson, ace of McGraw's staff, had outpitched Chief Bender, striking out eleven. It was his fourth straight World Series triumph over the Athletics, dating back to 1905.

On October 16, southpaws Eddie Plank of the A's and Rube Marquard of the Giants were locked in another pitching duel. The score was tied 1–1 until the sixth when, with two out, Eddie Collins doubled and Baker drove a home run over the right-field fence. The A's won, 3–1.

McGraw was furious with Marquard for throwing the home-run ball to Baker. "What the hell kind of pitch was that?" stormed McGraw. Before Marquard could reply, McGraw added disgustedly, "A good pitcher isn't supposed to give up a home run in such a situation."

That was the first World Series in which ghostwriting for ball players was done on a big scale and both Marquard and Mathewson had ghosted articles done for them about the Series for rival newspaper syndicates. Mathewson's ghost, Christy Walsh, tore the hide off Marquard in Mathewson's signed newspaper story the next morning. He accused Marquard of careless pitching and failure to follow orders. At a clubhouse meeting, the article explained, Manager McGraw had gone down the A's lineup and explained exactly what should and should not be pitched to each batter —Baker among them, of course. Obviously, Marquard had given Baker just what he wanted.

The next day, October 17, the Series returned to the Polo Grounds and Mathewson was back on the mound for the Giants, facing Jack Coombs, the third member of Connie Mack's Big Three. Both sides realized this was the key game of the Series and that the winner probably would go on to become world champion. The game went eleven innings. For eight innings, Mathewson was superb. The Giants had gotten a run for him in the third on hits by Chief Meyers, Matty himself and a grounder by Josh Devore.

Left: Rube Marquard, who threw gopher ball to Home Run Baker to lose the second game of 1911 World Series. Above: Frank Baker.

Going into the ninth, Mathewson still held his 1–0 lead. Dangerous Eddie Collins was an easy out on a grounder to third baseman Buck Herzog. Matty was now just two outs away from victory. The A's appeared doomed. They had managed only one run off Mathewson in forty-four and a third World Series innings. For him to yield a run, let alone a home run, at this stage, was unthinkable. The ubiquitous Baker was the next batter. Matty got two quick strikes on Frank. Both were low curves that came over knee-high. The left-handed batter swung at the first, and umpire Bill Brennan called the second.

Pitching deliberately and taking a slow, decisive windup, Matty let go the next pitch. Baker swung and the ball sailed into the right-field seats. The home crowd of more than thirty-seven thousand sat in a daze. The score was only tied, but the home run had a psychological effect on everybody, the players on both teams as well as the fans. There was a dreadful sense of premonition that this Baker blow portended an Athletics' victory. The premonition proved correct. The A's won in eleven innings, scoring two unearned runs on errors by Art Fletcher and Herzog and singles by Collins, Baker and Harry Davis.

Baker's game-tying homer off Mathewson gave Marquard and his ghost a chance to get even. Frank Menke, writing under Marquard's by-line, really taunted Mathewson for failing to hold his 1–0 lead.

"Will the great Mathewson tell us exactly what pitch he made to Baker?" Marquard asked. "I seem to remember that he was present at the same clubhouse meeting at which Mr. McGraw discussed Baker's weakness. Could it be that Matty, too, let go a careless pitch when it meant the ball game for our side? Or maybe Home Run Baker just doesn't have a weakness?"

The next seven days it rained. The teams didn't play again until October 24. And each day the writers referred to the A's' third baseman as "Home Run" Baker. The nickname stuck. Especially when the A's went on to win the World Series, four games to two—with Baker's home runs providing the winning margin in two of those victories.

A coolness developed between Mathewson and Marquard and it lasted all the way through the 1912 season, in which Marquard ran up his famous nineteen-game winning streak. They finally patched things up, but it was never again the same between them.

127

Giebell Pitches Tigers Into World Series—2-Run Shot in Fourth Stops Indians

FELLER'S 3-HITTER IN VAIN

Floyd Giebell's Moment of Glory

In one hundred fifty minutes the Detroit Tigers would come to grips with the Cleveland Indians in the most important game of the season, one of the most critical games in the Tigers' history. Manager Del Baker was acutely aware of the situation as he called his players together for a pregame clubhouse meeting.

The Tigers had come into the final week of the season in a deadlock with Cleveland and New York for first place. They had forged slightly ahead with three straight victories, and with three days of the schedule remaining, they needed a victory over the Indians coupled with a Yankee defeat at the hands of the Philadelphia Athletics to clinch the flag.

But they were in deep trouble. They were playing the Indians in the Tribe's own ball park before a hostile Ladies' Day crowd that liked to shower opponents with fruit, vegetables and other missiles. Also, this unforgettable afternoon,

they faced Bob Feller, who was enjoying the finest season of his career.

To make matters worse, Baker had run out of starters. His Big Three—Bobo Newsom (21-5), Schoolboy Rowe (16-3) and Tommy Bridges (12-9)—were arm-weary. All three had volunteered to pitch this big one but Baker was not sure. Besides, he had a hunch.

"I'd like to start Giebell," Baker told his players, "but I'll let you make the selection."

The players' choice was— Floyd Giebell.

Who?

He was a twenty-five-year-old right-hander, who had reported to the Tigers' training camp in the spring of 1940 but was soon sent down to the Buffalo club of the International League. After winning fifteen and losing seventeen at Buffalo, Giebell had been recalled by the Tigers less than two weeks before the season's end. He had made one start and had won.

Now, with a pennant as the carrot, the young man from the small community of Pennsboro, West Virginia, found himself facing the great Feller, who had already won twenty-seven games during the season. Showing unusual poise and confidence, Giebell kept pace with the blazing Indian fireballer through three scoreless innings.

The partisan crowd demonstrated its animosity in the first inning, flinging debris at Hank Greenberg as the Detroit left fielder set himself for a fly ball. Birdie Tebbetts, the Tiger catcher, was felled by a rubbish-filled basket and had to be helped to the dugout.

The public-address announcer pleaded with the fans to exhibit good sportsmanship. Giebell refused to be upset.

The Tigers broke through in the fourth. After a walk to Charlie Gehringer, Feller fanned Greenberg, but Rudy York slashed at a fast ball and drove it into the left-field seats for his thirty-third home run of the season. Roy Bell and Kenny Keltner singled in Cleveland's fourth but Giebell struck out Ray Mack to end the threat.

The rookie's most anxious moment came in the seventh, but again he was equal to the task. A single by Mack, an error by the usually sure-handed Gehringer on Rollie Hemsley's grounder, and Feller's sacrifice put Indian runners on second and third with one out. Giebell took a deep breath, fanned Ben Chapman and disposed of Roy Weatherly on a routine grounder to third baseman Mike Higgins.

Giebell experienced no further trouble, disposing of the last six batters in order. Detroit didn't score after the fourth but no more runs were needed. In all, Giebell allowed six hits, walked two and struck out six. Feller himself permitted only three hits, but they were enough to give the Tigers the flag.

Ironically, Giebell was not eligible for the World Series. In fact, his dramatic triumph turned out to be his last as a major leaguer. The following season Floyd appeared in parts of seventeen games but was never again involved in a major-league pitching decision. The 1941 season was the last for Giebell. He never appeared in a big-league uniform again. For one shattering moment, Floyd Giebell appeared in the spotlight, only to be forgotten before the last echo of applause had died out.

129

Joyful Tigers following pennant victory. From left: Billy Sullivan, Giebell, John Gorsicon, Del Baker and Rudy York.

BROOKS BEAT PHILS IN FOURTEENTH, 9-8

Robinson's Homer With 2 Out Decides Thrilling Uphill Struggle for Dodgers

Jackie Robinson Gives the Dodgers a Reprieve

It is ironic that Jackie Robinson tasted a moment of great glory in a year the Brooklyn Dodgers fell apart and lost a championship they had all but wrapped up. His heroics came in the final game of the regular 1951 campaign. Because of Jackie's triumph the dying Dodgers stayed alive a few days longer before finally succumbing to the New York Giants in the three-game play-off Bobby Thomson climaxed with his home run.

Jackie, who broke the color bar in baseball, may or may not have been the greatest all-around ball-player Brooklyn ever had. But there is no doubt he was the most exciting, fiercest competitor ever to wear a Dodgers' uniform. He created havoc on the bases. He carried a flaming spirit into every contest. He took risks that were shunned by other players. His mere presence on the base lines was enough to upset the opposing pitcher. He was a tiger in the field and a lion at the plate. He was at his best when it counted most.

The Dodgers' dissipation of a thirteen-and-a-half game lead in August was not the fault of Robinson. He batted .338, the second highest average of his remarkable ten-year career with the Dodgers, and, as usual, was toughest in the clutch. But, like the rest of the Dodgers, he kept looking back with dismay and disbelief as the Giants edged nearer—and finally there was no longer any need to look back. On Friday, September 28, two days before the end of the season, the Giants were abreast as the Dodgers lost to the Phillies. On Sunday, September 30, it was still a tie. A crowd of 31,755 came to Shibe Park to attend the Dodgers' final rites. Many of the voluntary pallbearers brought portable radios with them. They wanted to be among the first to hear of the Giants' victory in Boston, while watching the Dodgers get pasted.

They heard it, all right. The news of the Giants' 3-2 victory came before the Phillies and Dodgers were halfway through their game. The roar that went up from the stands sounded like a death knell to the Brooklyn players, who found themselves trailing 6-1 at the end of three innings, their morale shattered and their ace pitcher, Preacher Roe, knocked out of the box.

The Dodgers fought back, however, pulling up to 8-5 in the sixth. In the eighth, pinch hitter Rube Walker doubled to score two runs, and Carl Furillo singled to drive in the tying run. Manager Charlie Dressen sent big Don Newcombe to the mound in the eighth, and the fireballing right-hander waged a scoreless duel with Robin Roberts, the Philadel-phia ace, through the next three innings.

The game went into the twelfth. Darkness was descending on the field, making it difficult to follow the flight of the ball. League rules then prohibited the lights from being turned on. In the last of the twelfth, Philadelphia loaded the bases with two out. A hit, a walk, an error or a wild pitch would squash the Dodgers' pennant hopes. Eddie Waitkus hit one on the nose and sent a low line drive to the right of second base. Robinson raced over in the gloom of darkness and made an impossible diving catch inches off the ground. Few people realized that Robinson had caught the ball. A Western Union telegrapher, certain the ball had gone through to the outfield for the winning hit, punched out a message over the wires: "Dodgers lose. Giants win pennant."

The desperate catch jarred Robinson. He fell hard on his shoulder and collapsed. Anxious team-mates clustered around him as he lay on the ground. It was several minutes before Jackie rose groggily and walked uncertainly toward the dugout.

The game continued to the fourteenth. This would be the last inning. Roberts seemed to be getting stronger. He easily disposed of the first two batters in the top of the inning. Roberts got one ball and one strike on Robinson. Jackie stroked the next pitch and the ball streaked into the upper left-field stands for a dramatic home run and a 9-8 Brooklyn lead.

The Phillies still had three out to go and their number 2, 3 and

4 hitters were due to bat. Richie Ashburn opened with a single and was sacrificed to second. Bud Podbielan, who had replaced Newcombe in the thirteenth, bore down and disposed of the dangerous Del Ennis on a fly. Again it was Waitkus' turn to hit. This time he lifted an easy fly to left. Andy Pafko squeezed the ball for the final out and the Dodgers had their reprieve.

Clockwise from left: Manager Charlie Dressen with Robinson after the victory; Robinson with wind knocked out following game-saving catch in the 12th; Robinson being congratulated scoring winning run.

ATHLETICS' 10 RUNS IN 7TH DEFEAT CUBS IN 4TH SERIES GAME

Trailing, 8-0, Mackmen Unleash Attack That Beats McCarthy's Men, 10-8, Before 30,000.

15 MEN BAT IN ONE INNING

The Great World Series Comeback

132 The 1929 Philadelphia Athletics ended one dynasty and started another. It was to last three years, exactly the same length of time as the one the A's had ended, that of the 1926–28 New York Yankees.

The Athletics, led by wily Connie Mack and fueled by future Hall of Famers Al Simmons, Jimmy Foxx and Mickey Cochrane, not to mention the greatest left-handed pitcher of them all, Robert Moses "Lefty" Grove, made a cakewalk of the 1929 race after just missing in 1928. Their 104 victories were 18 lengths better than the winning total registered by the runner-up Yankees.

The Athletics demonstrated the same deadly efficiency in the World Series against the Chicago Cubs with their awesome collection of right-handed hitters: Rogers Hornsby, Kiki Cuyler, Hack Wilson, Riggs Stephenson and Woody English. Philadelphia won the first two games, 3–1, behind Howard Ehmke, then hammered out a 9–3 victory.

The Cubs won the third game and the next day shelled Jack Quinn, Rube Walberg and Eddie Rommel, building up an 8–0 lead with their ace, Charlie Root, pitching unbeatable baseball. The Series was on the verge of being deadlocked and who could tell where the Cubs would go from there? Jimmy Dykes, who played an outstanding game at third base for the Athletics that afternoon and collected three hits, remembers that game as if it had been played yesterday.

We were licked when we came to bat in the seventh inning. They had us 8–0 and Root was pitching like a machine. We hadn't been able to do a thing with him, and the way he was going it didn't look as if we were going to. As a matter of fact, it looked so hopeless that I found out later that Mr. Mack had made up his mind to let the regulars take their turns at bat in the seventh and then put in all the youngsters who hadn't ever been in a World Series. But they never got to play.

The A's were so completely resigned to losing that game that when Simmons opened the inning with a home run, the only comment anybody on the bench made was, "Well, we won't be shut out, anyway." Nobody got very excited even when Jimmy Foxx and Bing Miller and I followed with singles. Foxx was driven in, but Philadelphia was still six runs behind. Then Joe Boley scored Miller with another single. Five runs were still a lot of runs to overcome, especially in a World Series game.

And, when George Burns, batting for Rommel, popped to English, it looked as though the fun was over.

But Max Bishop banged another single for a fourth run, cutting the Cubs' big bulge in half and the fans began to sit up and take notice. Could Philadelphia overtake the Cubs after all? Joe McCarthy, the Chicago manager, must have thought so, because he took Charlie Root out and brought in his crafty southpaw, Art Nehf, to pitch to Mule Haas, batting left-handed.

What happened next turned Shibe Park upside down. Haas hit a line drive over second base; Hack Wilson started for it, seemed suddenly blinded by the sun, ducked away and the ball shot past him into deep center. By the time Kiki Cuyler had run down the ball and relayed it back to the infield, Haas had followed Bishop and Boley across the plate. Now the A's trailed by only one run, 8–7.

All of us had jumped to our feet, yelling. As Haas slid across the plate, I clouted the player next to me and shouted, "We're back in the game, boys!" Only it wasn't a player I hit; it was Connie Mack. I had never seen him leave his seat during a game before. But here he was, standing up, leaning out of the dugout, watching Haas race to the plate. And when I smacked him, I knocked him clear over the bats. "I'm sorry," I told him as I helped him to his feet. He smiled, reached out, patted me on the arm and said in that quiet way of his, "That's all right, Jimmy. Everything's all right. Isn't this wonderful?"

It wasn't over yet. Nehf, obviously rattled, walked Cochrane. That brought Sheriff Fred Blake to the mound. Simmons greeted him with a hard single for his second hit of the inning. Foxx followed suit and Cochrane joyously scored the tying run. McCarthy called in Pat Malone and he hit Miller with a pitch. Dykes came up with the bases full and promptly smashed a drive to left field. Stephenson leaped for the ball but it skidded off his fingers for a two-base hit, scoring Simmons and Foxx with the ninth and tenth runs of the inning.

Malone struck out the next two, but we weren't worried any more. Mr. Mack had brought in Lefty Grove to protect our two-run lead, and when Lefty went into a ball game it was all over. We knew he would set 'em down, and he did—six in a row, and struck out four.

The game ended 10–8. There is no inning in baseball to match that rally. Few doubted that the A's would win the next day and wrap up the world championship, which they did.

Hall of Famer Jimmy Foxx crossing plate in first game of Series. Foxx's power led A's to victory in the first game at Chicago.

BLUNDER COSTS GIANTS VICTORY

Merkle Rushes Off Base Line Before Winning Run Is Scored, and Is Declared Out.

CONFUSION ON BALL FIELD

Chance Asserts That McCormick's Run Does Not Count— Crowd Breaks Up Game.

The Boner That Cost a Pennant

134

It is sixty-three years now since the day Fred Merkle failed to touch second base. There are those who insist that the real villain of the drama that cost the Giants a pennant and sent the Cubs into the World Series was Hank O'Day, the umpire. Others have laid the blame on the doorstep of the National League president, Harry Pulliam. Regardless, Fred Merkle acquired a nickname that clung to him to his final day: Bonehead.

The other principals in *l'affaire* Merkle were Johnny Evers, John McGraw, Al Bridwell, Floyd Kroh, Joe Tinker and Joe McGinnity.

McGraw, the fiery manager of the Giants, vehemently insisted that his team was "robbed out of the 1908 pennant by a technicality." After piecing together all facts and versions of the incident, it seems that fate really worked overtime against the Giants, weaving an almost unbelievable web of coincidence and circumstance to enmesh the National Leaguers.

Fate made its first move before the rival teams ever took the field. Fred Tenney, the Giants' regular first baseman, who had played in all but one of the Giants' 157 games that year, awoke with a backache and sat out his only game of the season. Had Tenney been fit to play, the unfortunate Merkle, a nineteen-year-old rookie, would have remained on the bench. As for circumstance, it was nineteen days earlier, at Pittsburgh, that the Cubs were involved in a similar incident, this time with the Cubs as the losers.

The Cubs' magnificent Mordecai Brown was engaged in a scoreless mound duel with the Pirates' Vic Willis on September 4, with the Bucs at bat in the bottom of the tenth. Fred Clarke, the Pirates' player-manager was on third, Honus Wagner on second and rookie Warren Gill on first with two out when Chief Wilson singled sharply to center, scoring Clarke with the winning run. But Gill failed to run to second base. As was the custom of the day, whenever a runner scored the winning run, the other runners would immediately leave the diamond and head for the clubhouse. This time, however, the Cubs' brainy little second baseman, Johnny Evers, called for the ball from outfielder Artie Hofman. Evers got the ball, touched second and called for umpire Hank O'Day to rule it a force play for the third out, thereby nullifying the Pirates' run. O'Day refused to listen to Evers' plea. When the Cubs lodged an official protest, O'Day testified that he was so occupied with the runner crossing the plate that he did not see whether or not Gill touched second; but he added that if the play should occur again, he would watch for it and call it.

The flag race remained neck and neck and only percentage points separated the two clubs when the Cubs and Giants met before twenty-five thousand fans at the Polo Grounds on September 23. Giant-killer Jack Pfeister, a southpaw, opposed the Giants' immortal Christy Mathewson. And as fate would have it, O'Day was the plate umpire with Bob Emslie on the bases. The Cubs drew first blood in the fifth when shortstop Joe Tinker hit a home run. It was a low liner that Mike Donlin missed, trying for a shoestring catch. Donlin made amends in the sixth when he drove Buck Herzog home with a single. The score remained 1–1 as the Giants came to bat in the last of the ninth. After Cy Seymour went out, Artie Devlin singled to center and was forced by Moose McCormick. Up came Merkle and he slapped a hit to right, sending McCormick around to third. Al Bridwell was the next hitter and he singled to center. That's where the fun began.

Merkle headed for second but veered his course and sprinted for the clubhouse as soon as he saw McCormick touch the plate. The ever-alert Evers was waiting for just that. Here is Evers' version:

I was sure Merkle was a force-out at second if I could get the ball and tag the base before he woke up to the blunder. I yelled to Hofman,

our center fielder, to throw me the ball. Hofman, unable to see me clearly due to the crowd swarming on the field, threw the ball over my head. Joe McGinnity, who was coaching for the Giants and who realized what I had in mind, ran for the ball and picked it up. Joe Tinker, our shortstop, tried to wrest the ball away from McGinnity but the coach was able to pull away and throw the ball into the crowd. A spectator picked it up. Kroh, one of our pitchers, grabbed the ball from him, gave it to Tinker, who flipped it to me. I stepped on the bag and made sure O'Day saw me. "The run does not count," O'Day announced and

Clockwise from above: Hank O'Day, Fred Merkle and Johnny Evers.

walked away. Emslie refused to take a stand.

McGraw gave an entirely different version.

Evers did not get the ball. It rolled through the crowd and past third base. A Chicago pitcher, Kroh, grabbed the ball, but McGinnity snatched the ball from Kroh and threw it into the left-field bleachers. Evers never had the ball. He grabbed one of the spare balls from O'Day's pocket, ran to second, stepped on it and demanded that Merkle be called out. He appealed to Emslie, the base umpire, but Bob ignored the plea. Frankly, nobody paid attention to the squabble. We even joked about it in the clubhouse.

135

With the crowd milling all over the field, no attempt was made to continue the game. Manager Frank Chance of the Cubs claimed a forfeit because the home team could not clear the field. McGraw sharply protested that the Giants had won the game on the field. That evening, after conferring with National League president Harry Pulliam, who had attended the game, O'Day announced that Merkle was out, the run did not count and the game was a tie. Pulliam, in an official statement the next day, upheld O'Day's decision. President John T. Brush of the Giants appealed to the NL Board of Directors, who upheld Pulliam's ruling and ordered the Giants and Cubs to play off the contest on October 8, the day after the regular season ended.

With thirty-five thousand on hand, the Cubs, behind Mordecai Brown, defeated a weary Christy Mathewson, 4–2, giving the Cubs their third successive National League pennant.

September 29, 1954

Willie Mays' No.1 Catch

136

Ask Willie Mays what catch was the most important he ever made.

No contest. The catch I made on Wertz in the opening game of the 1954 World Series.

That's the defensive gem people remember best, the money catch that turned the World Series completely around, the catch that took a triple or a possible home run away from Vic Wertz, kept the Cleveland Indians from winning 4–2 in nine innings, and gave the New York Giants a chance to score their 5–2 victory on Dusty Rhodes' pinch-hit home run in the tenth inning.

Ask Willie what catch gave him the most satisfaction and he will talk about the same game, innings later. Mays' catch on Wertz was the most publicized. It was a great catch and Willie doesn't minimize it. It was a 2–2 tie in the eighth inning with the Indians at bat; runners were on first and second with nobody out. South-paw Don Liddle was brought in to pitch to the left-handed Wertz. Vic landed on the first pitch and smashed a terrific line drive toward deepest right-center, far over Mays' head. It looked as if the ball was bound for the bleachers, 460 feet away. Willie turned and ran full speed with his back to home plate and finally caught up with the ball a few feet from the wall. He had his arms stretched out in front of him, his glove up—and the ball fell into the glove while he was on the dead run. But the play was not over yet. Although off-balance, he turned and threw almost in one motion. Davey Williams took the throw in back of second, preventing the runner on second from taking more than one base. He died there, as the next two batters were retired.

I got a lot of publicity out of that catch. Some writers claimed it was the greatest defensive play they ever saw in a World Series. The truth is, I made a greater defensive play two innings later and hardly anybody noticed it.

Oddly enough, it was against Wertz, too. The score was tied when the Indians came up in the tenth. This time, Marvin Grissom, a right-hander, was pitching. Grissom's best pitch was a screwball, which broke away from a left-handed hitter. Wertz got hold of one of those scroogies and slammed a long foul to the wrong field, left.

That should have convinced me, but for some reason or other I wasn't thinking and continued to play Vic in right-center. Maybe I was remembering that long drive he'd boomed a few innings back. Sure enough, Wertz slammed one up the

left-center slot. It was the toughest chance I had the entire Series. The ball was mean as it landed and hopped, and I had to play it at an angle. Running at full speed, I just managed to spear it one-handed and held Wertz to a double. Had it gone through, it would have been an inside-the-park home run.

Wertz never got farther than third. Rhodes' homer for the Giants in their half ended the game.

*Willie Mays goes to the wall to rob
Vic Wertz of possible home run
in 1954 Series. Catch was probably
most famous of all time, but Mays
said catch he made later was better.*

Brooks Bow to Blackwell, 4-0, Then Top Reds in 9-8 Slugfest

Cincinnati Ace Has Double No-Hitter in Sight With One Out in 9th, but Yields 2 Blows—Furillo Bats Across 7 Runs

Blackwell's Miss

138

From the very beginning, baseball scouts summed up Ewell Blackwell as: "The kid can't miss."

At nineteen he was blinding batters with his fast ball in the International League as he rang up fifteen victories with four shutouts for the Syracuse Chiefs. Later, in Germany, he was the talk of GI baseball. With the Cincinnati Reds in his first season, he was picked, along with Warren Spahn, for the Rookie All-Star staff for 1946. In 1947 he was rated by many experts as the game's No. 1 moundsman.

Among other achievements, Blackwell won sixteen consecutive games for the fifth-place, spotty-hitting Reds to put him in class with Smoky Joe Wood, Walter Johnson, Lefty Grove and Schoolboy Rowe and set a National League record for right-handed pitchers. In his second big-league season, he won twenty-two games and the experts predicted nothing short of Hall of Fame greatness for the lanky right-hander from San Dimas, California.

"Blackwell's the best I ever looked at," testified Hank Greenberg, an evaluation seconded by many. "He's the toughest guy in the league to hit," offered Johnny Mize, another long-distance slugger. The best

hitters backed away from Blackwell's buzzball. Even Stan Musial and Enos Slaughter, the superb southpaw swingers, came to fear the 6-foot, 5-inch string bean, who looked even longer because he packed only 185 pounds on his elongated frame.

Blackwell's best pitch was a sidearm fast ball with a dip that practically collapsed. With his long arms and buggy-whip delivery, he used to drive right-handers crazy—and back on their heels. "He looks like he's pitching around a tree," Ralph Kiner once complained. "You don't see the ball until it's by you. All you see is that darned long arm coming right at you. It's scary."

Blackwell's greatest pitching effort took place on June 18, 1947, when he hung a no-hitter on the Boston Braves despite the fact that manager Billy Southworth threw a left-handed Boston lineup at him. Blackie threw only ninety-six pitches and allowed only two runners to reach second base.

Four days later, Blackwell faced a once-in-a-lifetime opportunity to equal a coveted record: Johnny Vander Meer's two consecutive no-run, no-hit games. Modern major-league baseball was in its thirty-eighth season when Vander Meer

pitched a no-hitter for Cincinnati against the Boston Braves on June 11, 1938, and followed it with another classic performance against the Brooklyn Dodgers four days later. Before then, and since, almost one hundred fifty pitchers have opened the door to the diamond's Hall of Fame by pitching no-hit games. And only one, Ewell Blackwell, came close to matching Vander Meer's brilliantly sustained effort.

Strangely, Blackwell's no-hitter was against Boston, the club that Vander Meer had made his victim in his initial hitless classic. Stranger still, Blackwell's next assignment was against Brooklyn, against whom Vander Meer had pitched his second no-hitter.

A Crosley Field crowd of 31,204 turned out to see that June 22 doubleheader. Blackwell, who was seeking his ninth straight victory, was the first-game starter, and he was opposed by lefty Joe Hatten. Both pitchers were untouchable for four innings—not a semblance of a hit. Then Eddie Miller, Cincinnati shortstop, doubled in the fifth for the first safety. In the sixth, the Reds scored when Hatten hit a wild streak and walked four hitters.

Meanwhile, the Dodgers could do nothing with Blackwell. The seventh inning came and went with the Dodgers hitless. Then the eighth. Only three Dodgers had reached base, all on walks. The Whip was buzzing them in and the crowd roared with each put-out. There was excitement, too, in the press box, where the sportswriters had their record books turned to the page noting Vander Meer's achievement, and in the radio booths, where the broadcasters were beaming to the baseball world the story of Blackwell's attempt.

Left: Blackwell practicing. Above: Pitching to Jackie Robinson en route to an almost double no-hitter.

Cincinnati tallied three times in the eighth to give Blackwell a 4–0 lead as he faced pinch hitter Gene Hermanski in the top of the ninth. Hermanski sent a routine fly to Augie Galan, the left fielder. As the fans held their breath, up stepped Eddie Stanky, who had taken three called strikes in the first and fourth innings and grounded out in the sixth. Stanky took a called ball, swung at the next pitch and drove it on a straight line at Blackie's ample feet. The tall right-hander reached down—but too late, as the ball sped between his feet out toward center field. Eddie Miller dashed over and flung himself at the ball, but it went beyond his reach and Blackwell's bid for double no-hit fame went by the boards.

Al Gionfriddo then flied out for what would have been the third out. Jackie Robinson, the next batter,

looped a single just inside the right-field foul line. Carl Furillo closed the game with a grounder to first base. Blackwell won the game 4–0, but to this day he blames himself for his failure to join Vander Meer in the pitchers' paradise.

I should have fielded Stanky's ground ball and turned it into an out. I did get my glove down fast enough to get it. I misjudged the speed and hop and it passed through my legs.

Blackwell's hard luck didn't end there. A few years later, when he should have been at the peak of a great career, he was felled by a kidney ailment that soon forced him to retire from baseball. The experts had tabbed Ewell Blackwell as a man of diamond destiny. They had forgotten: sometimes there is little to choose between destiny and fate.

October 10, 1924

The World Series That Lost to a Pebble

Walter Johnson had waited a long time to get into the World Series—seventeen years, in fact. The pitcher generally recognized as the greatest finally got the chance when his Washington Senators captured the American League pennant, their first, in 1924. The whole country seemed to be whooping for Sir Walter when he faced John McGraw's Giants in the opener. But he lost, 4–3, in twelve innings and was routed in his next start, 6–2. His chance to win a World Series game had come, not once but twice, and he had blown both. Now there would be no more chances. Johnson's hopes of ever pitching a World Series victory were ended, even though the Senators fought back valiantly to deadlock the Series at three games each.

There were tears in Walter's eyes as he boarded the train to Washington, where the seventh and final game was to be played. He made himself as inconspicuous as possible, avoiding people because he did not want their sympathy. He was still depressed as he arrived at the ball park the next morning. Clark Griffith, the owner of the Washington club, tried to cheer him

up. "We're counting on you to pull us through today if we need relief help."

The night before, manager Bucky Harris had come to Griffith's home with a plan. "Tell me if you think I'm crazy," Bucky said, "but I've got an idea how we can get a big edge on the Giants tomorrow." Bucky unfolded his idea. "This Bill Terry is murdering us," he said, "and McGraw is sure to have him in there at first base if we start a right-hander. Terry loves right-handed pitching. He's got six hits in twelve times at bat so far against our right-handers. Against left-handed pitching McGraw will play George Kelly at first base.

"Here's my idea. George Mogridge is the fellow who figures to beat the Giants tomorrow, but if we start him and have to shift to a right-hander, McGraw will switch on us and bench Kelly for Terry. I'm going to start Curly Ogden, a right-hander, and that will get Terry in the lineup, and then I'm going to lift Ogden after he pitches

to one batter and put in Mogridge. McGraw won't leave Terry in there against Mogridge, and we ought to be rid of him for the day."

Griffith liked the idea. "If you've got nerve enough to try it, I'll go along with you."

The trick worked. After Ogden had pitched to two batters, Harris took him out and sent in Mogridge, a southpaw, who held the Giants until the sixth. With two out and Terry coming up, McGraw jerked his young first baseman and sent in Irish Meusel. Harris had done it. He had gotten Terry out of the game. But the Senators were still in trouble as the Giants shelled Mogridge for three runs to take a 3–1 lead. Firpo Marberry, a great relief pitcher, held the Giants at bay through the eighth. The Senators, in the mean-

Clockwise from left: Fred Lindstrom, John McGraw, Earl McNeely.

140

time, rallied for two runs in the bottom of the eighth to tie the score. Playing manager Harris, who had homered for the first Washington run, singled home the tying run.

Some thirty-two thousand people, including President Calvin Coolidge, were crammed into the park and all stood up to greet and cheer Walter Johnson when he walked to the mound to face the Giants in the ninth. Utter strangers were hugging each other in the stands because Walter was getting one more chance in the Series. It was his ball game now, with the score tied at 3–3. Johnson recalled that dramatic moment years later.

I didn't have much confidence in myself. I was thirty-six years old and that's pretty far gone to be walking into the last game of a World Series—especially when you've lost two starts already. Bucky must have noticed the look on my face when he handed me the ball. "You're the best we got, Walter. We've got to win or lose with you." I remember thinking, "I'll need the

breaks," and if I didn't actually pray, I sort of was thinking along those lines.

Walter was in trouble in every inning. After he got Freddy Lindstrom in the ninth, Frankie Frisch hit a fast ball to right-center for a triple. Walter struck out George Kelly, who had succeeded Terry at first base, and retired Irish Meusel on a grounder to third. Johnson walked Hack Wilson in the tenth, but got Hank Gowdy to hit into a double play. Heinie Groh singled in the eleventh and was sacrificed to second, but Johnson fanned Frisch and, after purposely walking Ross Youngs again, he struck out Kelly for the second time. Meusel singled in the twelfth but Walter got the next three hitters. In the meantime, Jesse Barnes and Hughie McQuillan kept the Senators from scoring either.

Jack Bentley was on the mound when the Senators came to bat in the bottom of the twelfth. He retired the first batter and looked as if he had the second one, too, when Muddy Ruel lifted a pop foul behind the plate, but Hank Gowdy, the Giants' catcher, stepped on his mask, stumbled and dropped the ball. Given a reprieve, Ruel doubled past third. Travis Jackson fumbled Johnson's easy grounder to short, bringing up Earl McNeely. McNeely bounced one sharply, but straight, to Lindstrom—an inning-ending double play, for sure. Fred never touched the ball, however. It hit a pebble and bounced over his head.

I turned and saw Ruel crossing the plate. Tears were in my eyes. We'd won. I'd won. I felt so happy that it didn't seem real. They told me in the clubhouse that President

Coolidge kept watching me all the way into the clubhouse. A long time later Mrs. Johnson and I slipped away to a quiet little restaurant where I used to eat on Vermont Avenue in Washington, and you know that before we were through with our dinner, two hundred telegrams had been delivered there.

141

AGEE GETS HOMER, SCORES THIRD RUN

Eludes Tag in Close Play In Sixth—43,274 Watch Cubs Lose 5th in Row

When Tommie Agee Shattered the Cubs

In 1914 there were the miracle Braves, who rose from last place in mid-season to win the National League pennant. In 1951 there was the miracle finish of the New York Giants, who fought back from a thirteen-and-a-half-game deficit on August 13 to defeat the Brooklyn Dodgers in a pennant play-off a month and a half later. In 1969 there was the real miracle team of the age—the New York Mets.

Historians will point out that the year before they won the pennant the Braves were in fifth place. The Giants, a perennial contender, finished in third place in 1950 and were picked by many experts to win in 1951. But the maligned Mets were not given a ghost of a chance to finish in the first division in 1969. Ninth place, the year before, was the highest plateau they had reached.

No team had ever gone from ninth place to a pennant and a World Series victory the next year. Once the Boston Red Sox went from ninth to first, but the St. Louis Cardinals knocked them off in the 1967 World Series.

Always, in such miracle finishes, there is a particular set of circumstances game analysts will point to as the key. To the Mets and their followers the key was the series of encounters with the Chicago Cubs and a certain Mets' player by the name of Tommie Agee. Manager Leo Durocher and his Cubs, firmly entrenched in first place, weren't taking the Mets seriously in early July. Why should they? The Cubs had a fat five-game bulge on the Mets.

"Let's kill them off for good," Leo ordered his charges as they came into Shea Stadium. It didn't quite turn out that way. The Mets won two out of three. Tommie Agee, in the midst of a remarkable comeback after a dismal first season with the Mets, was the key figure in the Mets' victories. Tommie led off one game with a triple and another with a home run against right-hander Bill Hands.

"Wait till we get 'em in Wrigley Field," said Ron Santo, the Cubs' third baseman and leading run producer.

But it was no different in Chicago's home park. The Mets again won two out of three. In the finale, a 9–5 Mets' rout, Agee again led off with a hit, a double off Ferguson Jenkins, to ignite a four-run first inning.

Now it was September 8 and the Cubs were invading Shea Stadium for the last time. They still possessed a two-and-a-half-game lead over the Mets. A Cubs' sweep of the two games would deflate the Mets and almost surely extinguish their pennant hopes. Leo Durocher entrusted Hands, his best pitcher, to drive the first nail into the Mets' coffin. He was opposed by left-hander Jerry Koosman.

Hands had received another order. Infuriated by Agee's lead-off heroics, which had produced three extra base hits—double, triple, homer—in their last five encounters, Durocher had made it plain to Hands that this must not happen again. Like a good and obedient soldier, Hands sent Agee sprawling into the dirt with his first pitch. An angry Agee responded by clubbing the next pitch out of the park. He also scored twice, including the winning run in a 3–2 triumph. The Mets, behind Tom Seaver, won again the next day, and Agee contributed two more hits. The Mets now trailed the Cubs by a half game. The following night the Mets swept a doubleheader from Montreal to take over first place. The Cubs were through. The Mets were not to lose to the Cubs again until the final day of the season after the pennant had been wrapped up.

The Mets won thirty-eight of their last forty-nine games, but the 3–2 victory on September 8, spearheaded by Tommie Agee, was the final turning point.

They were trying to run us out of the ball park. I knew they were mad about my lead-off hits. I think they came in and said, "Let's knock him down and see what happens."

Well, I don't mind being knocked down. If you're hitting they're going to knock you down. The only thing I don't like is if we don't retaliate.

143

Koosman took the hint. His first pitch in the second inning hit Ron Santo on the arm.

"It's a matter of survival," Koosman said. "Agee doesn't have a chance to get even in center field. His way of getting even is through the pitcher. Eddie Stanky told us in the minors that if they hit your man hit three of theirs."

Agee said he wasn't rooting for Koosman to hit Santo, but it did not exactly make him break down and cry.

I'm not going to stick my neck out for a pitcher who won't protect me. When he protects me it gives me great incentive to win for him.

Tommie Agee not only won for the pitcher, he won for the entire club. In the third inning, with a man on, he hit his twenty-sixth home run. In the sixth, right after the Cubs had tied the score, he doubled to left and scored the winning run on Wayne Garrett's single.

Tommie Agee slides safely across home with winning run in crucial game against Cubs. Durocher protested that Agee was out, but to no avail.

October 13, 1921

Great World Series Climax

Thrilling finishes in the World Series are not rare. For instance, Bill Mazeroski's ninth-inning home run that broke a tie for Pittsburgh against New York in 1960; Bobby Richardson's catch of Willie McCovey's line drive with two out and the tying and winning runs on base in the ninth, giving the Yankees a victory over the Giants in 1962; Earl McNeely's ground ball that hit a pebble and bounced over Freddy Lindstrom's head to bring home the winning run in the twelfth inning for a Washington triumph over the Giants in 1924.

One man's choice of the most thrilling Series finish is the double play by the Giants in the ninth inning to defeat the Yankees in the first post-season contest between the New York teams in 1921.

Eddie Brannick, who was bat boy for the Giants when the immortal Christy Mathewson pitched three shutouts against the Athletics in the 1905 World Series, now in his sixty-seventh year with the Giants, picks this as the greatest of all World Series plays.

By this time, I had become assistant secretary of the Giants. I can remember all the detail of the play. The Giants in those days used to have New York pretty much to themselves, and the Yankees were the club that played in the Polo Grounds when the Giants were on the road. But they got Babe Ruth in 1920 and their attendance soared.

They continued to pack them in at the Polo Grounds, our ball field, in 1921, and though we had a good season, the Yankees had a better one. Both clubs won their pennants in close races. I don't think Mr. McGraw ever wanted to win a World Series as badly as this one, and we felt the same way all through the organization. We just had to win this Series. It would mean a lot for our old prestige to hang that world championship blanket from the center-field flagpole.

Well, the start was one of the flattest we've ever had. Carl Mays shut us out in the first game, 3–0, and Waite Hoyt, formerly one of our rookie pitchers, beat us in the second game by the same score. And what made it even more painful for Mr. McGraw was that Mike McNally stole home on us in the first game and Bob Meusel did the same in the second. That was just adding insult to injury.

In the third game, the Yankees knocked out Fred Toney and rang up four runs in the third inning before we scored our first run of the Series. But then we knocked out Bob Shawkey with four runs and went ahead in the seventh with eight runs to win, 13–5. We tied the Series by winning the fourth game, but Hoyt beat Art Nehf in the fifth, to put the Yankees ahead again.

Babe Ruth developed an abscess on his left elbow and was out of the last three games. He had collected five hits in fifteen times at bat with one home run, but the Giants' pitchers had struck him out eight times.

The Giants won the sixth and seventh games to take the lead for the first time. They were then playing for the best out of nine games and one more victory would clinch the championship for the Giants. The eighth game brought back Nehf and Hoyt to the mound. Though Nehf had pitched effectively, he had lost twice as the Giants could do nothing with Hoyt. They didn't score an earned run off him in three games.

Nehf held on to a 1–0 lead, holding the Yankees to four hits, while the Giants were making only six off Hoyt. The Giants had scored their run early and got it without a hit. After George Burns was retired, Dave Bancroft walked, Frankie Frisch fouled out but Ross Youngs walked on a 3–2 pitch. George Kelly hit a grounder to Roger Peckinpaugh, but the shortstop let it go through him and Bancroft crossed the plate.

It was still 1–0 when the Yankees came to bat in the top of the ninth. The first batter was Babe Ruth, no less. He was pinch-hitting for Wally Pipp.

I remember the Babe coming out of the dugout, his elbow all

145

bandaged. He had trouble swinging the bat and was an easy out. Aaron Ward then worked Nehf for a pass. That brought up Home Run Baker. Frank was thirty-five by then but he was still a good hitter. I had good reason to remember him. He had hit home runs on successive days, against Rube Marquard and Christy Mathewson, that won the 1911 World Series for the Athletics. That's how he got his nickname.

Well, Baker worked the count to 3–2 and sizzled a grass cutter toward right field. It looked like a sure hit. Johnny Rawlings, who had played great ball throughout the Series, made a great try for it. He barely stopped the ball in short right field, and fell down as he did so. But from a sitting position, he got the ball away and just barely nipped

Baker at first base. He had no chance at all to make the force play at second, as Ward had run on the pitch and was already rounding the bag by the time Rawlings got the ball.

Ward never stopped running. Believing the ball had gotten through, he rounded the bag and continued toward third. Kelly, catching sight of him from the corner of his eye, got the ball off almost the moment he tagged first to retire Baker. George had a great arm, but he never shot the ball across the infield with more on it. Frankie Frisch practically took the throw on his knees, and then tagged Ward just as he was sliding into third.

With both players sprawled on the ground, Frisch raised his hand to show the ball to Ernie Quigley and

Mike McNally steals home in first game against the Giants. Bob Meusel repeated crime the next day.

the umpire called Ward out. Some of the fans were so stunned by the sudden ending that they sat glued to their seats, not realizing it was over.

Second to first to third! How's that for a Series-ending double play? It happened and it made the Giants the new world champions.

Joe DiMaggio's 56-Game Streak

146

Baseball's greatest hitting streak was established by Joe DiMaggio, the most consistent ballplayer of his time. Like all good things, it had to come to an end, but not before he had lifted his team by the bootstraps from a position among the also-rans to the very top of the heap.

The hitting streak, nominated by experts as the greatest single accomplishment in baseball history—topping Babe Ruth's sixty home runs and Johnny Vander Meer's consecutive no-hit games—started innocently enough on May 15 when DiMaggio hit a single in four times at bat off a Chicago White Sox left-hander named Edgar Smith. The day before, against Mel Harder of the Cleveland Indians, DiMaggio had been hitless in three official times at bat. The Yankees were in fourth place, playing .500 ball. It wasn't until two months and three days later that Joe went hitless again. Ironically, it was Cleveland pitching again that stopped him.

In between those two hitless days, DiMaggio collected at least one safety in each of fifty-six consecutive contests. This remarkable streak,

longest in major-league history, lasted for more than one-third of the normal major-league schedule of 154 games. In that fifty-six-game span, the Yankees won forty-one and lost thirteen for a .759 percentage to climb from fourth to first place, and they wrapped up the pennant on September 4, the earliest clinching in history.

In a very real sense, DiMaggio had carried the Yankees on his broad back. They came alive when the streak became a day-to-day headline and they never stopped winning.

Baseball people did not take notice until the streak reached twenty-five. Press boxes all over the league kept track as the streak continued. Even Joe began to get interested when he passed Rogers Hornsby's National League record of thirty-three games. On June 20, after he had stretched his streak to thirty-nine, Joe came up against a pitcher who had vowed to stop him. Joe recalled the moment:

Johnny Babich had tried out with us and the club sent him down. Then, in 1940, he caught on with the A's and he beat us five times. It cost us a pennant. Well, he was still sore, and he seemed to think that if he stopped me, even if he walked me four times, he'd be rubbing it in.

The first three pitches to me were high and wide. I got the hit sign, but I couldn't have reached the fourth pitch with a ten-foot pole. The second time up, it was ball one, ball two, ball three. But now he gave me one I could get to, and I knocked him on the seat of his pants. It went for a double.

The next day, in Washington, there was a doubleheader and DiMaggio tied and broke the American

League record of forty-one held by George Sisler. Now all that was left was to set his sights on Wee Willie Keeler's nineteenth-century mark of forty-four straight in 1897, when Baltimore was in the National League. DiMaggio left Keeler's mark behind when he homered off Heber Newsome of the Red Sox to make it forty-five games in a row.

Now DiMaggio felt release from the tension and he got even hotter, collecting twenty-six hits in his next forty-three times at bat. The streak was now fifty-six games long. A crowd of 67,468 were on hand when the Yankees met the Indians in Cleveland in a night game on July 17. Cleveland started a left-hander named Al Smith, and the first two times Joe drilled hot shots over third base. Somehow, Ken Keltner backhanded both drives and threw him out. The third time, Joe walked.

On his fourth trip, the bases were loaded with one out. Cleveland brought in Jim Bagby and this time Joe ripped a hot one to the right of Lou Boudreau at short. Lou set himself for it. The ball took a savage hop. Boudreau grabbed it bare-handed and whipped to second base, starting a double play.

The streak over, DiMaggio immediately started a new one. It carried for sixteen straight games. Just another little extra push to speed the Yankees on their way to their quickest flag clinching. Joe said:

The thing I'm proudest about that record is that every base hit was honest.

DiMag belts out 17th homer of the year in extending his famed hitting streak to the 39th day.

October 13, 1960

PIRATES WIN, 10-9, CAPTURING SERIES ON HOMER IN 9TH

Mazeroski Hit Beats Yanks, Lifts Pittsburgh to First World Title in 35 Years

Mazeroski's World-Series Winning Home Run

148

Every World Series takes its place in the annals of the National Pastime, but the 1960 post-season classic between the Pirates and Yankees must go down as the weirdest and whackiest of them all. The Yankees shattered records by the dozen and overwhelmed the Pirates in three games by the fantastic scores of 16–3, 10–0 and 12–0, yet when it was all over the Pirates were the world champions. The Yankees batted .338 as a club to .256 for the Pirates; they led in hits, ninety-one to sixty, and in home runs, ten to four, but when the chips were down it was a Pittsburgh home run that brought an end to the festivities.

Although they had won three of the first five games, the Pirates appeared to be near the vanishing point going into the seventh game. Only the previous day, the Yankees, behind Whitey Ford, had slaughtered Pittsburgh pitching for seventeen hits and won by a lopsided 12–0

score, and it appeared that the seventh game would merely serve to crown the Yankees again. There was no reason to think otherwise as the game proceeded. The Pirates took an early 4–0 lead, but the Yankees, continuing their heavy onslaught, battered Pittsburgh ace Vernon Law off the hill and took a 7–4 lead.

The Pirates, however, had been battling back every Series game and were not about to give up now. Gino Cimoli batted for relief pitcher ElRoy Face and singled off Bobby Shantz to open the Pirates' eighth. Then came the big break of the Series. Bill Virdon rapped a grounder to the left of second base. Tony Kubek, the Yankees' shortstop, set himself for what appeared to be a certain double play. But once again, as it had happened in the 1924 Series when a bad hop skipped over Fred Lindstrom's head for a Washington victory over the New York Giants, the bouncing ball played a trick. Virdon's grounder jumped up and hit Kubek in the throat for a hit. Kubek was forced to leave the game. Dick Groat followed with a single, scoring Cimoli and bringing Jim Coates to the mound for the Yankees. Bob Skinner sacrificed the runners along. The tying runs were in scoring position, but the runners were forced to hold up on Rocky Nelson's short fly to Roger Maris.

For a moment the Yankees breathed easier, but Roberto Clemente beat out an infield hit, scoring Virdon. The Pirates were still one run behind. The picture changed seconds later when reserve catcher Hal Smith delivered sensationally with a home run that turned Forbes Field into a bedlam. Three

runs crossed the plate to give the Bucs a 9–7 lead.

But the Yankees weren't through. Bob Friend took the mound in the ninth in an effort to preserve the Pirates' lead and failed dismally when Bobby Richardson and pinch hitter Dale Long both singled. Harvey Haddix, coming to the rescue, retired Roger Maris but Mickey Mantle singled to center scoring Richardson. Then came a crucial play. Yogi Berra shot a sharp two-hop smash that Nelson backhanded just beyond first base. The force of the ball spun him around with his back to the plate. Rocky couldn't make a play on pinch runner Gil McDougald, racing home with the tying run. Instead he stepped on first to retire Berra, then looked toward second only to discover that Mantle was diving back to first. Nelson made a swipe at Mantle but missed and the score was knotted at 9–9.

As it turned out, all the Yankees' effort did was set up one of the most dramatic moments in World Series history. Ralph Terry was now the Yankees' pitcher and his first delivery to Bill Mazeroski, the Pirates' lead-off hitter in the ninth, was a ball. The next pitch was one that endeared Mazeroski to Pittsburgh fans forever.

I can still see that pitch today. I was looking for a fast ball and it came in chest high—just right. The thing I didn't want to do was overswing. I'd been up in the seventh inning with a runner on first and one out and I had tried too hard. I wasn't after a home run then, but I did want to hit the ball hard and I overswung and grounded into a double play. This time I really

wanted a home run, but I thought about that double-play grounder and had to remind myself not to overswing.

He didn't. The ball carried some four hundred feet over the wall in left-center and hundreds in the

Forbes Field crowd of thirty-six thousand fans were out there trying to shake Mazeroski's hand before he crossed the plate. It was the most timely home run in World Series' history and made the Pirates the champions of the world.

149

Bill Mazeroski bounds home after hitting 9th-inning home run to capture World Series for Bucs.

*Hartnett's Homer
With 2 Out in 9th
Beats Pirates, Puts
Cubs in First Place*

Gabby Hartnett's Home Run in the Dark

It was an afternoon that beggared description, an afternoon of glory in the life of a stouthearted Irishman who, as darkness almost hid him from the sight of nearly thirty-five thousand quaking fans, changed the map of the baseball world with one devastating blow.

Only the day before the Cubs, with Dizzy Dean on the mound, had defeated the Pirates to climb to within a half game of the league-leading Bucs. Now, a second straight time, Gabby Hartnett was standing after the game in a club-house filled with teammates fighting for words, staring at one another, pushing Gabby back and forth.

Billy Herman was in the middle of the floor, arms akimbo. When he could talk it was a hoarse whisper of awe, "Lord God Almighty." Billy wasn't even swearing. He was simply asking the heavens above to confirm that this thing he'd just seen with his own eyes had truly happened.

It had been a Pirates' day until the Cubs rallied in the late innings. When Hartnett came to the plate in the ninth there were two outs. Quickly the count went to two strikes against him. One more out and a tie game would be put over for a doubleheader the next day because

it was no longer possible to see in the gloom. Then came the next pitch, Gabby's swing—and the booming home run. Far out in the stands a mailman caught the ball, and even while Hartnett struggled in the arms of his men, the mailman appeared in the clubhouse with a plea for Hartnett's name.

Give him a new one and I'll sign it. I want to keep this one forever. I've now had the greatest thrill of this old life.

It was a game for the gods— a game that climaxed a stirring comeback by the Cubs. Only ten days before, the Pirates had held what seemed to be a comfortable three-and-a-half-game lead. Now, as Clay Bryant faced Pittsburgh's Bob Klinger, the Pirates' lead was a slim half game. Nine pitchers trudged to the mound that day as first one team and then the other took the lead. The tide of battle surged bitterly through breaks, good and bad.

The Pirates, smarting and in a vengeful mood, finally went ahead, 5–3, with two runs in the top of the eighth. The Cubs roared back in their half of the eighth, scoring twice before they were stopped by Mace Brown's relief pitching and a brilliant throw by outfielder Paul Waner, which cut down the lead run at the plate.

It had been a dark afternoon. Now it was getting difficult to see. The umpires conferred. They decided to let the teams play one more inning. Charlie Root retired the Pirates easily in the ninth. Brown disposed of the first two Cubs' batters in the bottom of the ninth. Old Tomato Face, who had succeeded Charley Grimm as manager in the

middle of the season, was the next hitter. One more out and the game would be called. This is the way Gabby remembers it:

I swung at the first pitch and missed. I swung again and got a piece of it for a foul and strike two. I had one more chance. Brown let fly again and I swung with everything

I had and I got the kind of feeling you get when the blood rushes to your head and you get dizzy. A lot of people have told me they didn't know the ball was in the bleachers. Well, I did—maybe I was the only one in the park who did. I knew it the minute I hit it. When I got to second base I couldn't see the bag for the players and fans there. I don't think I walked a step to the plate. I was carried in. But when I got there I saw George Barr [the umpire] taking a good look—he was going to make sure I touched the platter.

The Cubs were in first place. The pandemonium among Hartnett's teammates and the frenzied roar of the hysterical partisan crowd told the whole story. And while the pennant was still to be won, the Cubs could not be denied. They won again the next day, 10–1. The heart had gone out of Pittsburgh. The Cubs clinched the flag the following day, the Pirates broken by Gabby Hartnett's "home run in the dark."

Hartnett takes a swipe during batting practice and (far left) is mobbed after homer in dark.

October 10, 1926

JOYFUL CARDINALS PRAISE ALEXANDER

Thevenow Won Game, Veteran Pitcher Saved It, Manager Hornsby Declares.

Alexander Fans Tony Lazzeri

152

Grover Cleveland Alexander registered 373 victories, tying Christy Mathewson for the most National League games ever won by a pitcher. He won thirty or more games three successive seasons. He hurled four one-hitters in one year and turned in sixteen shutouts in a single campaign.

Rogers Hornsby owns the highest lifetime batting average of any right-handed hitter. His .358 lifetime mark includes three .400 seasons, one of which was the unexcelled .424 in 1924. Yet both of these Hall of Fame immortals maintained that the peak of their respective careers came on the same day, in a game in which Alexander pitched fewer than three innings of relief and Hornsby contributed two meaningless singles.

The game in question took place on October 10, 1926. It was the seventh and final game of the World Series between the New York Yankees and the St. Louis Cardinals. Hornsby, in the prime of his career, had taken over the managing reins of the Cardinals that year and guided them to their first National League flag. The thirty-nine-year-old Alexander, at the twilight of his career, had been acquired in mid-season by the Cards, on waivers from the Cubs, and

had helped pitch them into the World Series.

After Herb Pennock had beaten the Cards' Willie Sherdel 2–1 in the opener at New York, Hornsby called on Alex. He whipped Babe Ruth and Company, 6–2, retiring the last twenty-one Yankees in order. When the Series moved to St. Louis, the Yankees won two out of three and came back to the stadium with the pleasant prospect of merely splitting even to win the title. They might have made it, too, if it hadn't been for Alexander. Old Pete rose up to beat them in the sixth game, 10–2, to even the Series at three-all.

It was now or never for both teams and it was here that the Alexander World Series legend began. Jesse Haines, the ace of the Cardinals' staff, started against Waite Hoyt, and even though the knuckle-ball expert had pitched the Series' only shutout, Hornsby was taking no chances. Early in the game he turned to Alexander and said, "Alex, go down to the bullpen and keep your eye on Sherdel [Willie] and Bell [Herman]. Keep 'em warmed up and if I need help I'll depend on you to tell me which one looks best."

The Yankees got a run in the first, but the Cards came back with three in the fourth on singles by Tommy Thevenow, Chick Hafey, Jim Bottomley and a couple of errors by the Yankees. Joe Dugan's single and a double by Hank Severeid gave the Yankees another run in the sixth. Haines was breezing along until the seventh when he suddenly developed a wild streak. With two out, he walked three men to fill the bases. Hornsby came out to the mound to

ask what had happened. Haines held out his hand. A blister had developed on the knuckle of the first finger of his right hand. The blister had broken and the raw spot was bringing pain with every pitch.

Now let Alexander pick up the rest of the narrative:

Well, I was sitting around in the bullpen, not doing much throwing, when the phone rang and an excited voice said, "Send in Alexander." I didn't find out what happened until the game was over. The bullpen in Yankee Stadium is under the bleachers and when you're down there you can't see what's going on out on the field. All you know is what you learn from the yells of the fans overhead.

So when I come out from under the bleachers I see the bases filled and Lazzeri standing in the box. Tony is up there all alone with everyone in that Sunday crowd watching him. I say to myself, "Take your time. Lazzeri isn't feeling any too good up there. Let him stew."

There have been all kinds of stories that I celebrated the night before and had a hangover when Rog called me from the bullpen to pitch to Lazzeri. That isn't the truth. After I had beaten the Yankees the

day before, Rog came over to me in the clubhouse and said, "Alex, if you want to celebrate tonight, I wouldn't blame you. But go easy; I may need you tomorrow."

I said, "OK, Rog. I'll tell you what I'll do. I'll ride back to the hotel with you and I'll meet you tomorrow and ride out to the park with you." Hell, I wanted to get that big end of the Series money as much as anyone. I had a few drinks at the hotel on Saturday night but I was cold sober when I faced Lazzeri.

I remember Hornsby handing me the ball and saying, "We're in a tough spot and there's no place to put this guy." "I'll take care of that," I told Rog. Bob O'Farrell, our catcher, came out to talk to me. "Let's start right where we left off yesterday," he said. Bob reminded me we'd gotten Lazzeri out four

straight times Saturday with the curve ball.

I said OK to O'Farrell, we'll curve him. My first pitch was a curve and Tony missed. O'Farrell came out again. "Look, Alex," he began. "This guy will be looking for that curve next time. Let's give him a fast one." I agreed and poured one in, right under his chin. There was a crack and I knew the ball was hit hard. A pitcher can tell pretty well from the sound. I turned around to watch the ball, and all the Yankees on base were on their way. But the drive had a tail-end fade and landed foul by several feet in the left-field bleachers. So I said to myself, "No more of that for you, my lad." Bob signed for another curve and I gave him one. Lazzeri swung where that curve started but not where it finished. Well, we were out of that jam but there still were two innings to go.

153

Alexander set the Yankees down in order in the eighth and retired the first two in the ninth. And then Babe Ruth came up. The Babe had accounted for the Yankees' first run with a tremendous homer and he was dynamite to any pitcher. Alex, pitching carefully, walked Ruth on a three-and-two count. Bob Meusel, a home-run hitter in his own right, was the next batter. On the first pitch to Meusel, the Babe surprised everyone by breaking for second. O'Farrell wasn't caught napping, though. His accurate throw to Hornsby had the Babe by ten feet.

I'll always remember putting the ball on him, Hornsby recalled. He didn't say a word. He didn't even look around or up at me. He just picked himself off the ground and walked away.

October 4, 1955

'PERCENTAGE' SET STAGE FOR AMOROS

Alston's Strategy Dictated
Shift That Moved Sandy
Into Big Role in Series

The Catch That Sent Brooklyn Berserk

There have been numerous memorable events, joyous and tragic, on this earth on the fourth of October. In 1861 on that day the Union Army massed for the battle of the Potomac; October 4, 1864, the Erie Railroad opened; October 4, 1940, Hitler and Mussolini met at the Brenner Pass. On October 4, 1944, the U.S. Army broke through the German West Wall. Al Smith, former governor of New York State and onetime Presidential candidate, died on that day in the same year.

As far as Brooklyn is concerned, the greatest day in history was October 4, 1955. That was the day Brooklyn, after seven fruitless tries, finally won a World Series— and from the Yankees, who had beaten them five straight times in the October classic. It is no wonder that from Greenpoint to Bushwick, Coney Island to Flatbush, people went berserk as only Dodgers buffs knew how.

At precisely 3:43 in the afternoon at Yankee Stadium, Pee Wee Reese's sure-handed throw beat Elston Howard for the twenty-seventh out, and the capacity stadium audience exploded with emotion. The entire Dodgers' team raced out on the field to maul, slap, hug and kiss the two men who had made victory possible: a broad-shouldered, blue-eyed, straw-thatched southpaw named Johnny Podres and a slight, sad-looking, stringy-haired, unheralded outfielder named Sandy Amoros. The Dodgers were world champions, having toppled baseball's most formidable barrier, the twenty-one-time American League champion Yankees.

When the Dodgers lost the first two games, the Borough of Brooklyn could have been properly called a disaster area. Strong men brooded over their beers in Red Hook and Canarsie saloons. They damned manager Walter Alston, and brought out record books to prove that no team that had lost the opening two games had ever recovered to win a seven-game World Series. With such vaunted sluggers as Mickey Mantle, Yogi Berra, Elston Howard, Moose Skowron and Hank Bauer in the Yankee lineup and two such pitchers as Whitey Ford and Bob Turley, what chance did the Bums have? The Dodgers didn't even have a set lineup. One day Alston would have Junior Gilliam at second base, the next in left field and sometimes he'd have Gilliam at both positions in the same game.

Along the Gowanus Canal, the buffs swigged and testified against Alston. Then Podres, on his twenty-third birthday, beat the Yankees in the third game, 8–3. The following afternoon, the Dodgers repeated, winning 8–5. It was all so wonderful, especially when rookie Roger Craig beat the Yanks, 5–3, to send the Dodgers ahead in games, three to two. Who cared that Ford came back to win his second game of the Series?

Now the stage was set in the final scene. It was Podres against Tommy Byrne. The Yankees' southpaw pitched well, but Podres was even better, especially in the clutch. Five times Podres found himself in a jam and each time he came through. The Dodgers drew first blood, scoring a run in the fourth on a two-bagger by Roy Campanella and a two-out single by Gil Hodges. In the sixth, Hodges knocked in a second run with a sacrifice fly. Having used a pinch hitter for Don Zimmer, Alston moved Gilliam from left field to Zimmer's second-base position and sent Sandy Amoros to play left field, which in Yankee Stadium is like asking a blind watchman to guard the treasury.

Amoros never was any ball of fire, either at bat or in the field. However, this was another day. It was the sixth inning, and Podres was in deep trouble. He had walked Billy Martin, and Gil McDougald had bunted safely. Two on and nobody out. Coming up were Yogi Berra, Hank Bauer and Moose Skowron. Berra was a well-known left-handed pull hitter. Amoros was playing him well toward center. And then Podres threw Berra a pitch that made him reach. Yogi promptly sliced it to the opposite field.

It had to be a double, at least, and good for two runs. Amoros had to run a good hundred feet or more toward

154

Sandy Amoros, journeyman outfielder, stabs ball going away before turning and throwing for double play.

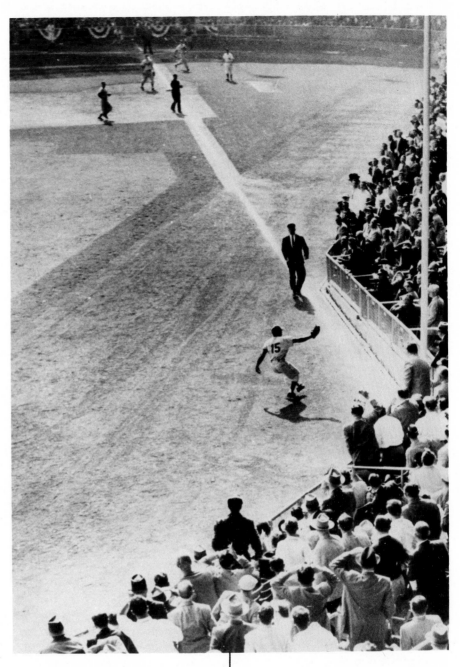

the slicing drive. Confident that it was going to drop safely—knowing Yankee Stadium as they did—Martin and McDougald took off like scalded cats. Martin pulled up but Mc-Dougald kept on going, practically breathing down Martin's neck. But behold, Amoros had out-raced the drive, grabbed the ball with one hand, no more than a foot away from the left-field barrier. The little outfielder braced himself on the barrier, wheeled and relayed the ball to shortstop Pee Wee Reese.

The two base runners were now forced to retrace their steps. Martin managed to get back to second base but Mc-Dougald, frantically trying to scurry back to first, was a dead pigeon as Reese's fine peg to first baseman Gil Hodges doubled him up easily. There was still Bauer to retire and Reese got him, too—simply an inning-out out.

Podres had to pitch out of still another jam in the eighth. Phil Rizzuto and McDougald singled around Billy Martin's out, but Podres retired Berra and Bauer to end that threat. The ninth was easy as Podres got Bill Skowron, Bob Cerv and Elston Howard in order. The Dodgers had been delivered into the promised land.

Tagging Two at the Plate on a Two-Bagger

156

Only a handful of catchers have had the good fortune to tag two base runners out at the plate on the same play. Luke Sewell, the one manager to lead the St. Louis Browns to an American League pennant, went a step farther. He accomplished the feat on the tail end of a two-base hit.

Luke remembers it well, because this once-in-a-lifetime play, according to the brother of the more famous Joey Sewell, created the spark that ignited his team—in this case, the 1933 Washington Senators—to drive to an American League pennant.

During a hot-stove league session at the 1970 Baltimore-Cincinnati World Series, Sewell said:

I'll never forget it. I've had many great thrills but this one remains my greatest.

Sewell did a lot of playing in 1933, catching 141 games for Joe Cronin's pennant-winning Senators. Sewell recalled the background of the event:

The Yankees were world champions, having beaten the Chicago Cubs four straight in the 1932 Series. My brother Joe was the third baseman on the club. Washington had finished third in 1932, but not many persons gave us much of a tumble as a contender when the 1933 season started. However, we got off to a good start, and were right behind the Yankees when we went into New York for our first 1933 visit to Yankee Stadium.

With George Pipgras pitching against Wally Stewart, the Yankees won the first game, 3–1, and a big Saturday crowd of thirty-five thousand fans were out for the second game, April 29. By assaulting Lefty Gomez for five runs in the fourth inning and knocking him out in the next frame, Washington went ahead, 6–3. The Yankees promptly scared the daylights out of Washington with an uprising that was quelled in fantastic fashion.

Monte Weaver was pitching for us, and the first four Yankee batters in the ninth made rousing hits, and still the Yankees were retired with only one run. Babe Ruth, first up, crashed a single to right, and his old running legs, Sammy Byrd, went in for him. Lou Gehrig sent Sammy to third with another poke to right, and Dixie Walker, then a promising Yankee recruit, kept it up with a third line single that scored Byrd.

That left Gehrig on second and Walker on first with none out, and the crowd yelling its head off. Cronin had somebody warming up, but as Weaver had held the Yankees to four hits in the first eight innings, Joe wanted to give Monte a chance to get out of the hole.

There was a great yell from the crowd as Tony Lazzeri hit a long drive to deep right-center. Goose Goslin took off after it, and Gehrig, playing it safe, remained near second to see whether he would catch the ball. It finally went over Goslin's head and hit the wall. Goslin played the rebound perfectly and made a long throw to Cronin. Because of his strong arm, Joe went out to handle the relay. He whammed in a perfect peg to me at the plate.

I could see the ball coming in, and out of the corner of my eye caught sight of Gehrig running down the third-base line. Maybe Lou didn't think the play was going to be close, as he didn't slide, and half-broke his stride just before he reached the plate. That's when I put the ball on him, and George Hildebrand called him out. Had Lou slid, I never could have tagged him. He hit me hard at the plate and spun me completely around. But as I spun, I caught sight of Walker coming down the line. I dove down the third-base line, blocking him off from the plate, and also tagged Dixie. I'd completed a double play, getting both put-outs at the plate. I do not know who was more crestfallen, the thirty-five thousand in the stands or the Yankee bench.

There was an amusing sequel to the big play. Lazzeri, who had reached second base, had stopped to watch the incredible happening at the plate. He was so stunned, he made no attempt to advance any farther. As Bill Dickey stepped into the batter's box, Sewell walked out to the mound, holding up two fingers.

"It's two out, Monte," he said.

"Oh, do we have two out?" Weaver asked.

Sewell looked quizzically at Weaver, then quickly turned his back to the pitcher so that Monte couldn't see his face break out into a grin.

I couldn't help laughing. Weaver probably was the best mathematician we had in baseball at the time. He later became assistant professor of mathematics at the University of Richmond, but here he couldn't add one and one.

The game ended a moment later when Dickey grounded out to Bob Boken at second.

That late April game did something for our club. We showed we weren't scared of the mighty Yankees and could beat them in their own park. It helped make the Washington club of 1933.

The Senators were back in August for a four-game series. The Yankees won the first two games, 6–5 and 5–4, one of them on an error by Cronin. It cut Washington's lead to one game. The Senators, however, bounced back, winning the next two, 5–1 and 4–1, to regain their three-game lead. Cronin broke up the last game with a bases-loaded triple. From then on, the Senators put a lot of daylight between themselves and the Yankees and eventually won the flag by seven games.

Left: Monte Weaver taking World Series warmups. Below: Luke Sewell, who tagged out two at home.

157

GIANTS CAPTURE PENNANT, BEATING DODGERS 5-4 IN 9TH ON THOMSON'S 3-RUN HOMER

Bobby Thomson: Dodger-Slayer

Andy Pafko stood in a state of shock at the base of the left-field fence, at the 315-foot mark near the foul line, and saw the ball sail into the seats above his head. The game was over. The season was over. One swing of the bat and all the work of the Dodgers over a stretch of 157 games was down the drain. He had seen it happen but it just couldn't be true. The Giants had won, 5–4.

For a while, the same state of shock engulfed all those 34,320 fans present at the Polo Grounds. Then reaction became upheaval. Now men, women and boys were standing up, screaming at the top of their lungs, delirious with joy. Others wept openly. Some simply stood with clenched fists, trying to scream from throats that could not produce a sound.

"Good God Almighty," one man said over and over.

On the field, the Giants were delirious in their acrobatics. The Dodgers had shrunk to ghosts.

As long as baseball will live, this game, which decided the 1951 pennant race in the National League, will also live. Those who were fortunate enough to be there on that historic afternoon will recount the final inning of this final play-off game, batter by batter, pitch by pitch. They may differ on how many men were on base, the count to the batter and whether the ball landed in the first, second or third row of the lower stands. But there will never be disagreement on the guy who hit the home run—the most timely, most important, most dramatic home run ever hit. If it can be truthfully said that one player ever won a pennant all by himself with a single swipe of his bat, then Bobby Thomson did it.

One swing climaxed the Giants' unparalleled drive that produced thirty-seven victories in their last forty-four games of the regular season to overtake a mid-August thirteen-and-a-half-game lead by the Dodgers. After winning the first play-off game and losing the second, the Giants had been held to four hits and one run by Don Newcombe in the first eight innings of the rubber game.

Alvin Dark's infield single leading off the last of the ninth had created faint hope. Don Mueller's single had moved Dark to third, triggering some enthusiasm from the crowd. The buildup had been temporarily dashed when clean-up hitter Monte Irvin raised a high pop foul for the first out. But Whitey Lockman's double had scored Dark, sent Mueller to third and set the stage for Ralph Branca's entry from the bullpen. Excitement gripped the crowd. Mueller had jammed his ankle sliding into third and time was called. Leo Durocher, the Giants' manager, took advantage of this breather to talk to his next hitter.

"If you ever hit one," Leo whispered hoarsely, "hit one now." Strangely, it had a settling effect on Thomson. Years later he recalled his reaction to Leo's advice:

I could see Leo was as excited as I was and it calmed me down. Going back to the plate, I said to myself, "You're a pro. Act like one. Do a good job." I was concerned only with getting a hit and keeping the thing alive.

They were carting Mueller off on a stretcher as Bobby turned from Durocher and went back to home plate. Bobby saw Branca walk to the mound to replace Newcombe. As Branca threw his warm-up pitches to catcher Rube Walker, Thomson waited. He had won the first play-off game with a home run but had been less than sensational in this third and final game. His blundering baserunning had killed one Giants' rally, and two grounders had skipped by him at third base in the Dodgers' three-run eighth inning. Bobby had something to make up.

He settled in his familiar spread stance. Branca kicked and threw a high fast ball for a called strike. The next pitch came in high, too, and Bobby met it cleanly and solidly. The ball was a quick blur rising toward left field. All the thousands inside the Polo Grounds and the millions outside held their breath. Bobby Thomson held his breath longer than anyone. When he saw the ball finally land with world-wide impact in the stands, he gasped, and continued to fight for his breath as he circled the bases. No hero anywhere, off or on a baseball field, received a more hysterical welcome when he crossed home plate, with every member of the Giants and half the spectators in the park trying to embrace him at once.

Exit Bobby Thomson, Dodger-slayer.

158

159

*Thomson displays gifts (right)
and runs for shelter after homer.*

YANKS' HOMERS OWE MUCH TO WEST WIND

Gomez, Before Game, Predicts "a Dozen" by Ruth and Gehrig —They Try to Make Good.

SIX HOME RUNS SET MARK

When Babe Ruth Called His Shot —Or Did He?

Nobody but a blankety-blank fool would have done what I did that day. I could have struck out just as well as not because I was mad and I'd made up my mind to swing at the next pitch if I could reach it with a bat. Boy, when I think of the good breaks in my life— that was one of 'em.

Everybody knows about the game; the day that Babe Ruth hit a home run off Charlie Root in Wrigley Field. It was the third game of the 1932 World Series and Ruth's home run, one of the fifteen he hit in World Series competition, gave him the biggest thrill of his life.

I want to set one thing straight. I didn't exactly point to any spot, like the flagpole. Anyway, I didn't mean to. I just sorta waved at the whole fence, but that was foolish enough. All I wanted to do was give that thing a ride—outa the park— anywhere. It was silly but I got away with it.

This was the Babe's last World Series, because the Yankees didn't win again until four years later and by that time the Babe was gone. The Babe always maintained he had three ambitions: to play twenty years in the major leagues, hit seven hundred home runs and appear in ten World Series.

There was bitter feeling in this 1932 World Series because Mark Koenig, whom the Yankees had traded to the Cubs, was voted only a half share by the Cubs. The Yankee bench jockeys were really on the Cubs for being "cheap" and the Cubs retaliated by putting the needle to Ruth.

The Series didn't last long but it was a honey. Pat Malone and Burleigh Grimes, who didn't talk like any Sunday-school graduates, outdid themselves in thinking up insults to shout at Ruth. "Big Belly" and "Balloon Head" were among the mildest.

By the time the two clubs arrived in Chicago for the third game, the Cubs were fit to be tied. They had dropped the first two games of the Series. Ruth had never played in Wrigley Field before, but in batting practice he hit nine balls into the bleachers. Observing several Cubs standing around with their mouths open, he yelled derisively:

I'd play for half my salary if I could hit in this dump all my life.

When the Babe came up for the first time, Andy Lotshaw, the Cubs' trainer, waved a towel at him and yelled: "If I had you on my team, I'd hitch you to a wagon." Ruth responded by getting hold of one with two on and parking it into the stands for a three-run lead. But the Cubs came back, and when the Babe came to bat again in the fifth, the score was tied at 4–4. Again came the cries of "Big Belly" and "Balloon Head" from the Cubs' bench. Ruth got them even madder by giving them the choke sign—the thumb and finger at the windpipe. That's when the Babe decided to go for broke.

I turned to Hartnett behind the plate and said, "If that bum [Root] throws one in here, I'll hit it over the fence again." I took two strikes. After each one I held up my finger and said, "That's one—that's two." Hartnett could

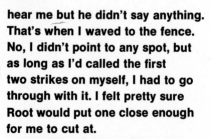

hear me but he didn't say anything. That's when I waved to the fence. No, I didn't point to any spot, but as long as I'd called the first two strikes on myself, I had to go through with it. I felt pretty sure Root would put one close enough for me to cut at.

I knew it was gone when I hit it. You can feel it in your hands when you've laid good wood on one. How that mob howled. Me? I just laughed, laughed to myself goin' around the bases and thinking what a lucky bum I was.

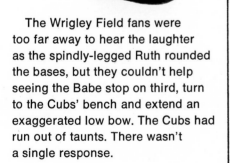

Babe Ruth (left) swings. Six years later he crosses plate. He is congratulated by Lou Gehrig following incredible predicted home run.

The Wrigley Field fans were too far away to hear the laughter as the spindly-legged Ruth rounded the bases, but they couldn't help seeing the Babe stop on third, turn to the Cubs' bench and extend an exaggerated low bow. The Cubs had run out of taunts. There wasn't a single response.

Haddix Hurls 12 Perfect Innings But Loses to Milwaukee in 13th

Pirate Southpaw Retires 36 in Row—

The Perfect Loss

He pitched twelve perfect innings, he retired thirty-six batters in a row, his teammates outhit the opposition twelve to one—and he lost. Impossible? In the case of Harvey Haddix, the impossible happened.

A pitcher hurls like this once in a lifetime—once in baseball history—and we can't win the game for him!

The speaker was Bill Virdon, who got one of the twelve Pittsburgh hits. Haddix did not give up his first hit until the thirteenth. But when he did, it ended a chance for baseball immortality.

Even the congratulatory telegram sent by National League president Warren Giles failed to soften the shock of a heartrending defeat for the little left-hander who had turned in one of the great pitching performances in baseball history.

There was little reason to think that Harvey Haddix would go the distance when the thirty-three-year-old farm boy faced lead-off batter Johnny O'Brien in Milwaukee's County Stadium that cold, dank night of May 26, 1959. Haddix hadn't been pitching well; his teammates hadn't gotten him runs in recent games. Adding to Harvey's problems was a hacking cough he had had for two weeks. The weather, cold and damp following an afternoon of rain, was no help. Neither was Milwaukee manager Fred Haney, who stacked the Braves' lineup with seven right-handed batters, including pitcher Lew Burdette. The only lefty hitters were Eddie Mathews and Wes Covington.

Using a fast ball and slider, the two pitches that would be almost his entire repertoire that night, Haddix quickly disposed of O'Brien. Mathews lined to first baseman Rocky Nelson, and dangerous Hank Aaron flied to center fielder Virdon.

Haddix's epoch-making performance was under way. Burdette, who had set the Pirates down in order in the first inning, yielded a hit but prevented Pittsburgh from scoring in the second. Haddix retired Smoky Burgess, Nelson and Bob Skinner in order. Inning after inning, Haddix and Burdette kept the opposing batters at bay. There was only one difference in their performances—Burdette was permitting the Pirates an occasional wasted hit; Haddix was pitching a perfect game.

Through the seventh and eighth innings the zeros for both teams kept going up on the big center-field scoreboard. Not a single Braves' player had reached first. But the Braves certainly were trying. In the third, Johnny Logan drilled a hard liner that Dick Schofield caught with a short leap.

In the sixth, Logan hit one into the gap between short and third, and Schofield again came to the rescue with a deft scoop of the grounder and a long throw.

It started to rain in the seventh but nothing seemed to bother Haddix. In the bottom of the ninth, Burdette was the batter. He yelled to Haddix, "I'll break up your no-hitter!" The count was two balls, two strikes. Burgess signaled for a slider. Harvey threw, Lew swung—and missed. County Stadium was bedlam. A perfect nine-inning game—but no victory. It had never happened before.

In the Pittsburgh tenth, Dick Stuart batted for Roman Mejias with one on and one out. He connected with a Burdette slider and sent a towering smash toward the center-field fence. Back . . . back . . . back went Andy Pafko and hauled it in just short of the barrier.

The crowd was with Haddix. He retired O'Brien in the tenth, becoming the first pitcher ever to retire twenty-eight men in a row. But until his teammates got him some runs, the frustration would continue. And continue it did—through the tenth, eleventh and twelfth. Haddix had made history again. No one had ever pitched a perfect game for more than nine innings; no one had ever pitched a no-hit game for more than eleven innings.

Burdette gave up his twelfth hit in the thirteenth inning but no run resulted. Haddix seemed tired as he came out for the thirteenth. Felix

Mantilla, who had entered the game in the tenth, hit a grounder to third. Don Hoak fielded the ball perfectly, but his throw bounced past Nelson at first. The official scorer ruled it an error and was cheered by the crowd. Mathews bunted Mantilla to second. Hank Aaron, the league's leading hitter, was purposely walked. It seemed like good strategy. Joe Adcock, the next batter, had struck out twice and grounded out twice. Haddix threw a slider, low and away. Ball one. Burgess called it again. Harvey wound up, threw, and as the ball left his hand, he wished he could have it back again. He realized the pitch would come in a little higher than he wanted it to. Adcock swung and the ball sailed toward the right-center field. Virdon went back to the wire fence and leaped frantically. The ball dropped over the fence for a home run.

At least, Adcock and everybody else in the ball park thought it was a homer—all but one. Aaron, who had touched second base, figured the ball had dropped at the bottom of the fence instead of over it, and calculating that Mantilla had already scored the game-winning run, he headed toward the Braves' dugout. Adcock, meanwhile, running with his head down, ran toward third base. Milwaukee players were waving to Aaron to go back and touch third and home, but Adcock had already passed him. The umpires declared Adcock out but allowed the two runs. The next day Giles nullified Aaron's run and ruled that the official score of the game was 1–0.

It was a bizarre finish to one of the most bizarre games ever played, a game in which a pitcher retired thirty-six consecutive batters— and lost.

163

Haddix pitches his perfect game, then is a picture of sadness following eventual defeat.

A dissection of and a getting into
baseball's components—
fielding, pitching and catching,
baserunning, hitting.

The glove men

fielding

by Charles Maher

Charles Maher is a sports columnist for the *Los Angeles Times*, where he has been for five years. Previous experience as a sports-writer includes jobs at the *San Diego Evening Tribune* and the Associated Press in Los Angeles.

There are times when the outfielder in baseball may seem to be little more than a uniformed spectator. You look out and he's just standing there, still as a statue. You figure if they didn't change sides between innings, he'd probably have birds nesting on him.

Earl Weaver has said: "People don't understand outfielders' skills. When you think of an outfielder like Paul Blair, who can be in full motion the instant a fly ball is hit, can take his eyes off the ball and still run right to the place where the ball is going to come down—to me, that is more remarkable than the anti-missile missile."

In the case of a good outfielder, this seeming absence of movement is misleading. While his body may be nearly motionless much of the time, his eyes and mind are seldom at rest.

That helps explain how Paul Blair can often get to where a fly ball is coming down without watching it in flight. "From center field," Paul says, "you can get a pretty good look at the swing of a hitter. You've got a straight-in view of the plate. If you watch close enough, you can usually tell which way the ball is going to go. If you see a right-handed hitter is getting out in front of the ball, you know the ball is going to go to your right, toward left field. If he hits the ball straight on, it's going to come out to you and if he swings a little behind the ball, it's going to go toward right field."

How can the outfielder tell the distance the ball is going to go?

"It's difficult," Paul says, "unless you concentrate. You have to see which part of the bat the batter hits the ball with. If he hits it around the label, the ball is not going to go very far. If he hits it on the fat part, you know it's going to carry.

"Some outfielders don't really watch the hitter with enough concentration. That's how you can get fooled on a bloop hit. You don't quite see where the ball hit the bat and when the batter follows through it may look as if he has hit the ball hard. You have a tendency to start back then. That's what lets a lot of balls drop in front of you. You can't just watch the swing. The swing is going to be about the same every time. It's where the ball hits on the bat that determines how far it's going to go."

So while the bat is the enemy's chief weapon, it also functions as part of Blair's early-warning system. Of course, he can't gallop away at the sound of the bat and proceed to the exact spot where the ball is going to come down every time. He may have to make a slight course correction after taking a quick fix on the ball late in its flight. But his early intelligence, acquired from watching the ball and bat as they meet, usually gets him going in the right direction.

To be sure, this intelligence would be worthless if Blair did not have good speed. It is one thing to know where the ball is going and quite another to get there ahead of it. But while speed is certainly a desirable attribute in an outfielder, Paul Blair would not have

Left: Hal Lanier comes way off base to avoid slide and throw to first. Above: Dick Green sidesteps Frank Howard and throws on.

169

Pirates' third baseman Richie Hebner fields ball with body in front and, with plenty of time, sets himself before throwing.

become the great defensive player that he is were it not for his invisible skills—his ability to concentrate and "read" the swing of the bat.

In fact, at any position in baseball, a player's ability to concentrate may often be as important as his visible skills. Occasionally, of course, even a very good player will do the wrong thing. And he may do it even though he has thought out the play beforehand and knows exactly what he should do. Second baseman Tommy Helms, who like Blair—and each of the other players quoted in this section—was named a defensive all-star by *The Sporting News* in 1970, tells this story on himself:

"Our club [Cincinnati] was playing Montreal one time and they had the bases loaded with one out in the bottom of the ninth. Tie score. Rusty Staub is the hitter. I'm telling myself I've got to go to home if the ball is hit to me.

"Sure enough, Staub hits a one-hop liner right at me. Mack Jones is going from first to second. When I get the ball, here is Jones, running right by me. So I reach out and tag him and then throw the guy out at first. We win the game in extra innings.

"I still don't know why I tagged Jones. If I wasn't going to go home on the play, I wouldn't have been playing in, right? Another thing I don't know is why Jones didn't pull up before he got to me, so I couldn't tag him.

"After the game, Gene Mauch [the Montreal manager] said to me, 'What would you have done if Jones had stopped running?' I said, 'I don't know. I guess I would have thrown home.' Mauch said, 'No, I don't think you would have done that. Maybe you would have done what I did one time in a situation like that. The runner stopped and I stuck the ball in my pocket. The game was over. We lost'."

A lot of people watching the Cincinnati-Montreal game probably thought Helms had made a very heady play when, in fact, he had pulled a rock that should have lost the game. He won't do that often. Broadway should have as many good plays as Helms makes in a season.

Tommy says he makes the good ones by following the advice of a former manager, Dave Bristol. "Dave always used to tell me to concentrate on making the routine plays. He told me that if you're conscientious about making those plays, the good plays will come. I believe him."

Like Paul Blair, Helms wants to know beforehand where the ball is going. He gets one clue by finding out what the next pitch is going to be.

"Suppose there's a left-handed hitter up," Tommy says. "If I see the catcher is calling for a breaking pitch, I might have my momentum going to my left because the ball is going to be thrown off-speed and the hitter is likely to pull it. If it's going to be a fast ball, I might take a step or two to my right. Getting a step or two like that can mean getting to the ball."

Jim Spencer of the California Angels plays first base

170

Outfielder Bobby Tolan runs down long out at Cincinnati's Riverfront Stadium.

and can't see the catcher's signs. But he gets help from his second baseman. "If there's a left-handed hitter up and the pitcher is going to give him a breaking ball," Jim says, "the second baseman will call my name in a low tone, so I can just hear it. That's a signal a breaking pitch is coming and I'll shade the hitter a little toward the bag."

There is probably no way of establishing what is the toughest play in baseball. But here are a few of the plays that a few of the best players like least:

Blair: "It's the line drive that's hit right at you. The problem is you can never tell for sure whether the ball is going to carry or dip on you. The way I try to differentiate between the two is that if I can see over the ball when it's about halfway out to me, I figure it's going to drop in front of me. If I can't, it's going to carry. The ball fools me now and then when it carries, but most of the time I've been lucky enough to be able to correct myself and get back so it isn't over my head.

"The next toughest play for an outfielder is when the ball is coming down close to the fence. You want to stay away from injuries and if you start running into cement walls that can be difficult. Fortunately, I seem to sense where the wall is without looking, and I'm able to stop a little quicker. Anyway, I haven't run into a wall yet."

Third baseman Brooks Robinson, Baltimore Orioles: "My most difficult play is probably going to my right. I think this is probably the toughest play for most infielders. A ball hit to your left is on your glove side and you can get your glove down in position to catch the ball at the last second. You just sort of throw the glove over there and get it open. But in going to the right, you should try to get the glove across your body while you're going after the ball. You should always try to go after the ball with the glove in position to catch it. The less movement you have to make at the last second, the better off you are."

Robinson talks about another play of which he has become the unquestioned master: "I guess a lot of people think the criterion of a good third baseman is how well he can come in on the bunt or the swinging bunt, where he has to pick up the ball and throw on the run. I always tell myself on a play like this that if the ball is coming to a stop, or is already stopped, I'll try to bare-hand it. If it's still rolling pretty good, I'll use my glove. The secret in making this play is catching the ball with your left foot forward. If you do that, you can be throwing on your next step, off the right foot. But if you come in and catch this ball on your right foot, there is no way you can throw that instant. [The arm is not yet in throwing position.] And you can't throw when your left foot hits the ground, so you have to wait until your right foot hits again and you're losing time."

Helms: "The toughest play has got to be the double play because you can't see the guy coming at you when you take the throw at second. You've got to be like a good quarterback and know when to eat the ball—I mean when to keep it instead of trying to throw to first. Sometimes you get a bad throw or you get hit and you shouldn't try to complete the double play because you'll have to throw off-balance and you might throw the ball away. I think in the last two years I've saved myself six or seven errors on knowing when to eat the ball. When I first started playing second, I thought I could make the double play every time."

Spencer: "I'd guess most people think the double play from first to second and back to first is the toughest play for the first baseman. But I haven't had too much trouble with this one. The toughest play for me is when the ball is thrown across the infield into the runner and I have to come maybe four or five feet down the line from first base to catch it, and try to tag the runner at the same time and still hold on to the ball. In the five years I've been playing professional ball, I've lost the ball about a half dozen times that way. Several times I've had my glove actually torn right off my hand and knocked down the right-field line. A couple of times after that happened, I couldn't move my arm the next day."

Below: Outfielder Carbo, making sure the ball won't get through, grabs it on the fly. Right: McCovey tosses the ball to Gaylord Perry at first, avoids a collision as the out is made on Hague.

172

Catcher Johnny Bench, Cincinnati Reds: "Blocking the pitch in the dirt and keeping the ball out in front is probably the toughest play for me. It takes a lot of alertness. You always have to be expecting a bad pitch. The ball will bounce different ways, depending on what spin it has on it. And it will hit the ground different distances in front of you. I don't know if you ever really get the hang of blocking the ball—I mean to the point where you can do it every time."

Bench thinks he has the toughest position on the field. "The catcher," he says, "has more things to do than anyone else. You've got pop fouls to go after, back toward the screen. You almost always seem to be going toward a potentially dangerous stationary object because almost any ball you go after is going to be out of play. Then you've got throws coming in to home and you've got to block the plate. And you've got to be able to field bunts, and call the game, and know the pitchers, and know the hitters, and block pitches in the dirt, and you've got to be able to throw out the runner trying to steal with a jump, and move the infielders and outfielders around, and try to keep up the pitcher's confidence." Apart from that, Bench says, the catcher is virtually without responsibility.

You might suppose that if you asked an outfielder which position is the most difficult, he would name one of the outfield positions, most likely his own. Not so. At least not if you ask Paul Blair.

"I think I might have the easiest position of all," Paul says. "The center fielder does have more ground to cover than anyone else. But most of the time the ball doesn't hook on you, the way it will on a left fielder or a right fielder. This is because the ball hit to center is hit squarely and it comes straight at you. Also, you can watch the ball coming off the bat better in center field. It's a little harder in left and right because you're at an angle to the batter.

"I would say shortstop and second base are the two hardest positions. You've got runners coming in on you on double plays and you can't watch them much. You can get hurt real easy there. I think the pivot is the hardest play to make—to avoid getting creamed and still get the ball away."

Helms: "The shortstop has the toughest job. People have a lot more speed than they used to have and the shortstop has got to make that throw from the hole. He can't ever bobble a ball or just knock it down and expect to get a man out. The hardest two positions have got to be short and second. You've got to be in on every pitch."

Spencer: "I'd say catcher. He's the quarterback in baseball. He has to control the game. He has to cover a lot of ground backing up first and third [a function Bench forgot to mention]. He has to set up the hitters and throw to the bases. I'm glad I'm a first baseman."

Robinson: "I'd have to say shortstop. You've got to

174

Cesar Tovar throws over Reggie Smith to complete double play.

have the best arm in the field, you have to have more range than anybody else and you're in the action on darn near every play."

You will get similarly divided opinions from others in baseball.

Ex-catcher Paul Richards, vice president of the Atlanta Braves: "I'd have to say it takes more ability to play shortstop well than it does to play any other position in any sport. A shortstop must have speed, agility, a great arm, instinct, the ability to come in and go out, to size up a play quickly, to be in the right place. Catcher is also a very important position to fill. If the ball starts going back to the backstop, you will start noticing the catcher. But you can be a catcher with no speed. You can be a catcher without being able to do anything but catch and throw, really."

Earl Weaver, Oriole manager: "Shortstop. You need the extra tools."

Ex-second baseman Billy Martin, manager of the Detroit Tigers: "I think second base, shortstop and catcher. Second base because of the double play, getting hit from the blind side all the time. Shortstop because of the fielding end of it. Catching because of the endurance end."

Ex-outfielder Harry Walker, manager of the Houston Astros: "You can't win without a shortstop and a second baseman who can handle the ball for you and you can't win without a halfway decent center fielder. But I think the catcher has the toughest job."

The argument, then, would appear to be beyond resolution—which puts it in the company of some of the best baseball debates.

Whatever position is the most difficult to play, Brooks Robinson will tell you all players have something in common when they are on defense: Their work is not fully appreciated.

"Most teams that win have good defenses," he says, "but the fielding is overlooked a lot of the time. The publicity all goes to the offense and the pitching. Hitting is what it takes to make a lot of money today."

Robinson says people come to take for granted the fielding of bad-hop grounders because major-league infielders manage to come up with so many of them. The difficulty of this play, he says, is certainly a lot greater than the amount of applause a fielder is likely to get for making it.

Spencer: "One play that might appear pretty easy for the first baseman to make is the scoop play, that is, when the ball is thrown into the dirt and you have to come up with it. You have to judge the speed of the ball. And you get all kinds of bounces because the distance the ball is from you when it hits the dirt varies. I'd rather have the ball land out a little way. The farther away it is when it hits the ground the more time you have to judge it. These plays are very difficult."

Richards: "Brooks Robinson made a play in the

Left: Although the outfielder has the call, second baseman Frank Quilici doesn't hear Oliva's "mine" and the two lose the ball. Above: Tito Fuentes leaps over sliding Tito Francona.

play-offs [1970] that a lot of people probably didn't really appreciate. It was a ball hit back up the middle and it bounced off the pitcher's arm or leg or something. Now the third baseman's normal reaction on a play like this is to wait until he sees the ball bouncing off the pitcher and then go after it. But Brooks has learned that when you see a ball hit toward the pitcher you don't wait. You run immediately toward the mound. That's what Brooks did in this case, and he gained enough steps by doing it to be able to throw the guy out. He does this all the time. It's one of the little things that make great plays."

Harry Walker talks about a play that does look hard, but not nearly so hard as it actually is: "The ball is topped between first and second. The pitcher is going after it and the first baseman is coming in. Now, how do they make the decision on who is going to cover first? Does the first baseman stay with the ball and the pitcher go over to cover first, or does the pitcher go for the ball and the first baseman to the bag? There is a lot of time spent on this play, but you'll see times when they'll both goof up. They'll both go for the ball or they'll both give up.

"I like to see it worked where the pitcher breaks toward a point about fifteen feet down the line from first base. If he can't field the ball, he keeps right on going and covers first. The first baseman can see the play developing. He can see whether the pitcher can get to the ball. If he sees the pitcher is not going to get it, the first baseman keeps coming. You can have the same play involving the pitcher and the third baseman when a ball is topped toward third with a runner on second."

Another play that may not be fully appreciated is the relay from the outfield.

Walker: "To me, one of the most exciting plays in baseball is when a man is trying to score from first on a double or is going for a triple. This means you have to have a lot of teamwork on defense. Say the ball is hit to right-center. If the center fielder and right fielder get to the ball at the same time, usually the man with the stronger arm takes over.

"Ordinarily, the second baseman will run into right-center. He'll be the relay man. How far does he go? It depends on how strong the outfielder's arm is, but a good standard procedure is that the first throw should be made a little more than halfway to wherever you're trying to get the ball.

"If the second baseman is the relay man, the shortstop will be the trailer. The trailer will line up at least thirty feet behind the relay man, to back him up in case the ball is overthrown."

Unfortunately, says Billy Martin, a lot of fans probably miss much of this elaborate defensive routine. "On the general relay play," he says, "the fan is watching the runner. He doesn't really get to see the play."

Sometimes you can get a better line on how a play is going to come out by watching a fielder than you can by watching the ball. Suppose, for example, that a high

drive is hit to deep center. It could be a home run. The center fielder races back. Ten feet short of the wall, he stops abruptly and turns back toward the infield. At that instant, you know the ball is not going to carry to the stands. The ball is still high in the air, but the fielder has told you it is going to come down at or near the point where he has stopped.

But a lot of people are not looking at the fielder. They are watching the ball. Most of them are not going to be sure where the ball is going until just an instant before the catch is made. They have been trying to measure how deep the ball was hit without really having anything to measure against. Their depth perception is not as reliable an indicator as the outfielder's movements.

There are times, however, when you can't trust

Dave Cash has time to throw before Randy Hundley's slide.

outfielders—as is illustrated by a story told by Paul Richards: "One time, when I was managing the Orioles, we were playing the Yankees in Baltimore. We were ahead, 1 to 0, but Mickey Mantle, their lead-off hitter in this inning, hit a line drive to right-center. Smoke and smog and fog were coming down over the field and it was difficult to see. Our center fielder, Jackie Brandt, saw he couldn't get to the ball. But he reached down and pantomimed picking the ball up and throwing it to second. Meanwhile, the right fielder, Russ Snyder, was going back to the wall to get the ball. He threw it in, trying to keep Mantle from making a triple. But Mantle was still on first. When Mickey looked out there in the haze and all and saw Brandt in the act of throwing, he figured Jackie must have somehow gotten to the ball. On the next pitch, we made a double play. We got out of the inning."

The quality of defensive play probably has risen in the past generation. The main reason is probably *not* that today's players are a lot better than yesterday's. It is because striking improvements have been made in equipment and playing conditions. One of those conditions, the defensing of a sacrifice bunt, is discussed by Earl Weaver in his section.

His comment on equipment: "When I started in baseball twenty-some years ago, they were using gloves without the fingers laced together and they had only two straps across the webbing. Gloves have been tremen-

dously improved. You can do a lot more one-handed fielding than in the past."

Richards: "The defensive part of baseball has probably made the most improvement since I started playing. The outfielders have learned to play the fences and the wind a little better, and the defensive techniques against the bunt have improved. But the big thing about fielding, the fundamental that major-league coaches try to teach today, is to be sure the infielder learns to get his glove open and facing the ball long before it reaches him. There have been successful infielders who kind of flipped their gloves at the ball at the last moment, but this took extremely fine timing. And when the player grew a little older, and his reactions grew a little slower, he began to miss the ball. If you get your glove open, you'll catch a lot of balls accidentally.

"This is the only thing a fellow named Brooks Robinson [who was signed by Richards] had to learn when he was a kid and changed from second to third base, which is another story. You know, Brooks doesn't run very well, but he is quick. And quickness is much more important

Below: Oakland's Dick Green makes tag on Solons' Ed Stroud and manages to hold ball. Right: Sal Bando beats Joe Foy's tag.

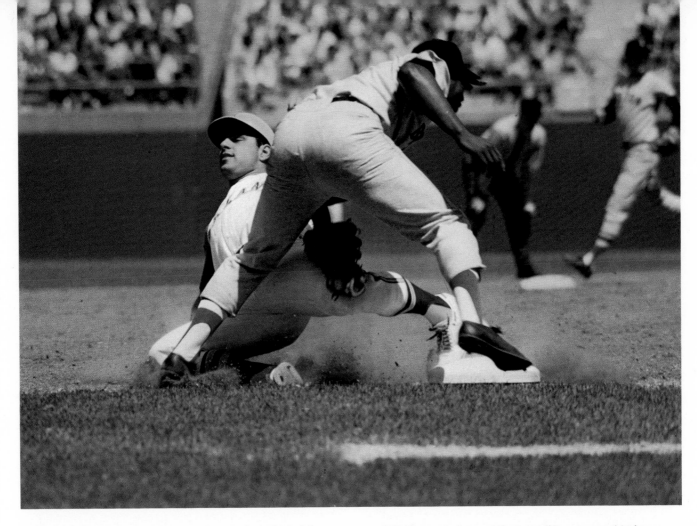

at third base than speed. This is why we thought he'd make a fine third baseman.

"But to get back to the way it used to be. We had a lot of groundkeepers in the twenties and thirties who were not as adept as groundkeepers are today. In recent years, even before synthetic turf started coming in, most infields were kept very smooth and bad hops were infrequent.

"Gloves, of course, have made a big difference. First basemen in the thirties wore gloves that barely fit their hands. Today the first baseman's glove is so large you can kind of throw it at the ball and the ball is likely to stay in there. With the glove a first baseman uses today, it is easier to catch a ball with one hand than with two. When we were coming up, they would tell us to learn to use both hands before we used one. Nobody taught the one-handed catch. Now you've got players like Rico Carty—I doubt very much if Rico would be able to catch a ball with two hands. He wouldn't know what to do with his right hand.

"Another thing about today's ballplayers: I think they're faster and quicker than they used to be, and there are more of them to choose from. Because of the increase in population, there are many, many more kids playing baseball than there were years ago."

Mauch: "When I was coming up, you used to catch the ball in the palm of your glove. Now, with these big gloves, the players snare the ball. At first I thought it was

unfair, because for a while everything seemed to be going against the hitter. But now that they're coming in with synthetic fields, and it's easier to get the ball through the infield, I think it's balanced out a little better."

Mauch says there is less emphasis on the defense today than there used to be. "Now," he says, "they figure the defense is on the mound. They try to build two things: pitching and power. That's about all they're really concerned with. They'll sacrifice a certain amount of defensive skill, figuring if their pitchers are strong enough they'll be able to pitch past any errors.

"I'm not saying everybody thinks that way. I'm still what you might call a defensive manager. But I think it's a trend. You take things like cutoffs, position play, moving on the count. Very few clubs are putting a lot of accent on them."

But others think more time is being spent in defensive training today.

Walker: "There is more teaching now than when I played. We have winter schools, the instructional league. There is a lot more time given to teaching. Hourwise, a ballplayer is exposed to three times as much instruction as he used to be."

Richards: "I would say this: Today, the ballplayers are trained. In the twenties and thirties, nobody paid any attention to them. You seldom got anybody to teach you the fundamentals. They just didn't bother with you.

They let you go back to the minors and teach yourself."

Martin: "When I was a kid coming up, they expected you to learn the hard way. Sometimes they wouldn't even let you take batting practice. I think it was more of an individual game then. Now everybody is helping. There's more specialized coaching going on."

Alvin Dark says there was more time spent on fundamentals twenty years ago than there is now. But he does not say today's player is poorly trained. "I think television has helped on fundamentals more than teaching," Dark says. "I think it's always better to teach by seeing methods than just by talking. Boys are taught certain things in Little League today and they can see the same things during games on TV. They learn from this. I think kids today are getting sound instruction."

Dark does not like synthetic playing surfaces. He says that they will lessen the value of the good defensive player. For instance, a shortstop with good range may be able to get to a ball hit into the hole on a conventional field. But synthetic fields are faster and if the same ball is hit on one of these fields, it will be through the hole before the shortstop can get to it. So his range is wasted.

"Another thing," Dark says, "is the bounce the ball takes on synthetic turf. It can go right over the infielder's head. The pitcher is taught from the time he comes into the game to keep the ball down. Now he'll make a perfect low pitch and on a synthetic field the ball will bounce over somebody's head.

"Or say there's a man on third and one out. Normally, you'd bring your infield in. But now you can't. The ball will bounce right over their heads.

"I think people get big thrills out of seeing players like Brooks Robinson make great plays. Put artificial turf in everywhere and there are going to be fewer of these."

Richards: "There are going to be more hits but no

Above: Brooks Robinson on his way to another fantastic stop. Right: Tony Perez puts the tag on Freddie Patek and Harry Wendelstedt calls the out. But Patek is unbelieving.

bad hops, so there will be fewer errors. Synthetic turf is going to put a premium on quickness. The ball is going to be by the infielder a lot faster, so he must be quicker than he would have to be on grass.

"Personally, I'd rather not see artificial turf. But I don't think the game will be affected materially from the fan's viewpoint."

Mauch: "In Cincinnati [where even the base paths are covered with AstroTurf] the fielder's background never changes. It's green from the time the ball leaves the bat until he catches it. They're simplifying it to the point where there's not going to be any premium on an infielder with speed [range]. Quickness of foot, for the first couple of steps, is what you're going to need. If you can't move quickly, you'll be out of business.

"I think a little more study is going to be put into playing position baseball. If you don't position yourself properly, you're just not going to get to as many ground balls. You've seen infielders that used to accept 1,000 or 1,050 or 1,100 chances in a season. They're not going to get to that many balls on synthetic turf."

But the players seem to like the stuff. Blair, Brooks Robinson, Helms, Spencer and Bench all make the point that synthetic turf guarantees the fielder a true bounce.

"Frank Robinson doesn't like it," Blair says. "The reason is, it hurts his legs to run on it. But everyone else I've talked to seems to like it. For one thing, you can charge the ball as hard as you want without worrying about it taking a bad hop. On a regular field, you may tend to hesitate a little more because of the possibility of a bad bounce. The only thing you have to worry about on artificial grass is that if it's a high pop it might bounce over your head."

Helms: "I don't think artificial turf is going to raise batting averages so much if the infielders adjust. You know, you can play back five or six steps farther than you can on grass. We play Stargell and McCovey and some of those guys way back. I mean way, way back. And you can still field the ball and throw them out because the ball gets to you so much faster than it would on a regular field. If those big guys don't hit the ball out of the park, it's going to be tougher on them.

"I think a second baseman can cut out five errors a year playing on artificial grass. I think everybody should have it."

In a few years, quite possibly, just about everybody will. But even if all the bad bounces are taken out of the game, there will still be some margin for error. A smooth field can't eliminate wild throws and dropped balls. And a good thing, too. For, as A. J. Gordon put it in "Ye Weary Wayfarer":

No game was ever yet worth a rap
For a rational man to play,
Into which no accident, no mishap,
Could possibly find its way.

182

Battery

pitching and catching

by Frank Slocum

Frank Slocum is a free-lance writer for magazines, radio and television. With Gil Hodges he is author of *The Game of Baseball*. From 1951 to 1965 he was Assistant to the Commissioner of Baseball.

Pitchers are very special people. There are factors that make them different from all other athletes. Perhaps the biggest of these differences is statistical. Pitchers are the only team sport athletes who are credited with victories and charged with defeats.

The quite natural result is that pitchers tend to have a proprietary interest in the games they pitch. This doesn't mean that they don't care about every game their team plays, but there is a great deal more concentration on the ones in which they are directly involved.

Just as the hitter quite often represents his team's entire offense when he steps into the batter's box, so does a pitcher often reflect the entire defense. In 1970, New York Mets' pitcher Tom Seaver, hurling in 291 innings, struck out 283 men. Nearly one of every three men Seaver retired in an inning, he retired by himself.

If it sounds as if the pitcher has a tremendous edge over the hitters, he does. He has an edge because he knows what the next pitch will be and the hitter doesn't. He also has an edge in the very basic area of mathematics. Ted Williams once said, "I've been exposed to pitchers all my life, making a living off their dumbness, off their mistakes." Williams did, indeed, make a living, and a good one, off pitchers, but let's look for a moment at the other side of the coin. Williams enjoys the distinction of being the only hitter in forty years to bat .400. It is indeed quite an accomplishment. But to a pitcher, the name of the game is getting the hitter out, and even a .400 hitter loses three times out of every five.

Pitchers get hitters out in different ways. Sometimes it's simply a matter of overpowering a batter. But basically the battle is one of wits. Warren Spahn has said—as have a lot of others—that pitching is an art.

Sandy Koufax said in his prime, "Every game I pitch, I start off with the basic idea of pitching a no-hitter. Once I give up the first hit, my goal becomes a shutout. Once they have scored a run, my goal is merely to win the game."

Robin Roberts wanted the opposition players to hit the ball. He believed that he had the law of averages working for him, and that the player would probably hit the ball where one of his teammates could catch it. Roberts, pitching with a substantial lead, was not a tough pitcher. Once the score tightened up, Roberts was a tiger. His primary consideration was to win, and the score by which he won was secondary.

Some pitchers take much longer between pitches than others. Their theory: The delay works against the hitter.

Other pitchers believe in working quickly. Bob Gibson is an example. He feels he gets better defensive support that way. "If a pitcher takes a lot of time, or if he throws a lot of pitches that are taken for balls by the batters, his infielders start to relax," he explains. "Maybe they're playing back on their heels instead of on their toes. By working quickly, I think I make my fielders more alert."

Whether they work slowly or quickly, all pitchers

must eventually face that moment when they let the ball go. That's the time when they have blended their mental and physical abilities into the act of pitching, and hope that neither has failed them.

A basic physical problem common to all pitchers is control, and it's here that the difficulties of pitching are best summed up. Control, to a pitcher, doesn't mean getting the ball over home plate, although that, by itself, can prove a challenge. A pitcher, from a distance of sixty feet six inches, must throw a ball over a target seventeen inches wide. And, unlike a dart thrower, he throws as hard as he can, often with a pulling, twisting motion so that the ball will change direction in flight.

Control, to a pitcher, means getting the ball not too high, not too low and, usually, not over the middle of the plate. Good pitchers don't feel that they have the whole plate to work with, only part of it. The late Fred Hutchinson used to describe certain pitches by saying, "It was the kind of pitch that the umpire would have called a strike if he'd gotten the chance. However, before that could happen the hitter had belted it out of the ball park."

In the days when Sal Maglie was one of the top pitchers in the National League, his talent was analyzed by Brooklyn Dodgers' coach Clyde Sukeforth: "Maglie's not going to overpower hitters, but he'll beat you with

*Orioles' Jim Palmer flashes classic form: ball hidden from view,
eyes always on target, high kick for momentum, the entire
body into the pitch, the follow-through and readiness to field.*

control. He doesn't bother with the middle fifteen inches of the plate. He just keeps the ball on the inside or the outside inch."

Warren Spahn says, "Hitting is timing. Pitching is upsetting timing." This is accomplished with several different kinds of pitches, but there can be no question that the most important of these is the fast ball. We hear a great deal about certain pitchers relying on other pitches, but basically that's not the case.

Take Mike Cuellar. Cuellar throws an outstanding screwball, which breaks sharply in the opposite direction from his curve ball. During the 1970 World Series, Sandy Koufax told a national television audience: "We hear a lot about Cuellar's screwball being his best pitch. It's not. His best pitch is his fast ball. Every pitcher's best pitch is his fast ball. It's the fast ball that makes the other pitches effective. Hitters must look for it and try to adjust for a breaking pitch. While they are looking for the breaking pitch, the fast ball is by them before they can adjust."

In his book, *The American Diamond,* the late Branch Rickey, whose knowledge of baseball was among the best respected in the game, spoke of different pitching styles.

"There are three kinds of pitchers in the major leagues. The first kind gives the batsman a problem with his stuff. He makes it hard to get the bat and ball middles together. He is a problem in the vertical zone—an imaginary one erected immediately in front of the plate. He is a speedster, a strikeout artist. He has stuff, managers call it. His name could be Walter Johnson. He doesn't need a screwball, a slow curve, a change of pace or a slider. Walter Johnson was not a pitcher in the generally accepted sense of the word. He was a thrower. All he had to do was rear back and throw the ball through the middle, and not often could the batter hit it squarely. This is one class of major-league pitcher: the Amos Rusies, the Cy Youngs, the Guy Bushes, the Ed Walshes, the Smoky Joe Woods, the Rube Waddells, the Lefty Groves.

"The second class are pitchers and not throwers. They need superb control and they are expert in varying velocity. A batsman anticipates a certain speed, starts his swing, but finds that the ball is not yet up to the plate. The next pitch gives the illusion of great speed in contrast to the previous one and is met well back of the plate. This kind of pitcher has changes of speed, perhaps two curves, a slider, a change-up off the fast ball, or a dipsy-do [the old-time parabola slow ball]. This sort of

pitcher also makes good in the majors: Carl Hubbell, Preacher Roe, Sal Maglie, Ed Lopat, Robin Roberts, Bobby Shantz and many others.

"The third group is simply a combination of the first two, and all pitchers of the present era try to belong to this class. They afford a hitting problem in both zones, the vertical and the horizontal. They may approach the Johnson fast ball and the Hubbell changes. They include such pitchers as Christy Mathewson, Grover Alexander, Dizzy Dean, Bob Feller, Kid Nichols, Jack Coombs, Burleigh Grimes, Eddie Plank, Whitey Ford, and, of course, many others. The really great pitchers largely belong to this third group."

As for the first group that Mr. Rickey mentions, the throwers, it's important to remember that the ability to throw with speed, even exceptional speed, is not enough. Unless the velocity of the pitch is really great, a pitcher cannot exist merely on a fast ball. Even with that great speed, there is the enemy of time to consider. On a given day, that speed may not last into the late innings of the game. (Here a good exception is Bob Gibson, who, on many occasions, seems to throw just as hard in the ninth or tenth inning as he does in the first.) Also, the years take their toll. The exceptional fast ball might sometimes be enough. The good, or even very good, fast ball is never enough.

The necessity of a good fast ball for a pitcher is something of an enigma because most hitters are fast-ball hitters. That is to say, the average hitters prefer to bat against fast balls. An outstanding exception is Willie Mays, who has always been a dangerous breaking-ball hitter. Yet here we are still talking about good fast balls, or even very good, but not about the exceptional ones.

The sign of the exceptional fast ball is its ability to "hop." The ball will come toward the plate and, at the last instant, tend to elevate. Pitchers whose fast ball "moves" can get away with throwing the ball at a level around the shoulders. However, with anything less than the outstanding fast ball, most pitchers prefer to keep the ball between the mid-thigh and the knee of the batter. The low pitch, whether it is a fast ball or breaking ball, is harder to hit when it's kept low for a simple reason: The higher the pitch, the easier the ball is to see and follow.

The value of the fast ball to the pitcher without exceptional speed lies in its being "showcased," as opposed to being a pitch used to get a hitter out. A pitcher may throw his fast ball deliberately out of the strike zone, merely to show it to the batter. Its primary purpose is to provide a contrast for the next pitch, most likely an off-speed delivery.

Basically there are four kinds of breaking pitches: the curve ball, the screwball, the slider and the sinker. There have been articles published to the effect that the curve ball is an optical illusion. Many years ago, a college professor who shared that view visited the spring training base of the New York Giants in Phoenix, Arizona.

Opposite: Classic mound form by Bob Gibson (top) and Dave Giusti.

He gave his reasons for not believing in the curve ball to the Giants' manager Leo Durocher, who listened and nodded. Finally, Durocher said to the professor, "I'll tell you what we'll do. We'll get a big flat piece of wood, like a door, and place it on the front line of the batter's box. You stand in the box, then I'll have one of my pitchers take a bag full of baseballs, walk out to the mound and beat your head soft with some optical illusions." The offer was gratefully declined.

The sinker is a curve ball that breaks almost straight down, as opposed to the usual angle of down and away from a hitter. The sinker is a much rarer pitch than the straight curve, although we've seen more of it in recent years. The same is true of the screwball. For some reason pitchers with outstanding sinkers today are, for the most

190

Two opposing pitching stances are shown by Mets' Tom Seaver and Angels' Tom Bradley. Seaver stretches his entire body to its limit before releasing. Bradley releases from upright stance.

part, relief pitchers. Perhaps the reason lies in the fact that throwing a sinker takes a tremendous toll on the arm, an impossible strain for more than a few innings at a time.

The slider falls somewhere in between the fast ball and the curve. The slider breaks, but not as much as the curve ball. It is, however, thrown with greater speed than a curve. It is probably the most controversial of all pitches. About the only universal point of agreement is that it's a relatively easy pitch to learn, although more difficult to perfect.

But is it good or bad? Mr. Rickey said that he didn't believe in it, and that it hurt more pitchers than it helped, his theory being that pitchers went to the slider rather than working to get better control of their curve ball. On

the other hand, Ted Williams says that all hitters have trouble with the slider and that he considers it the best pitch in baseball.

Good or bad, in the years since World War II it has become a tremendous factor. While there are people who say that the possibility of another .400 hitter was lessened by the influx of night games, Stan Musial takes a different viewpoint. He says, "When I broke into the big leagues, a hitter hardly ever saw a slider. Now it seems like everybody's got one. I know that some people like it and others don't, but that's not important. Hitters found it tough enough when they had to look only for a curve or a fast ball. At least they had a 50-50 chance of guessing right. Now the odds are lowered because of the slider."

With all breaking pitches, the danger lies in the failure of the pitch to break. Bob Gibson, in his book *From Ghetto to Glory,* says, "Usually I will not throw a curve ball after the sixth inning. When you're tired, that's when a curve ball is dangerous. You're not pulling down on it as hard as you should and it hangs. A hanging curve is a pitch that's hit for a home run."

While it's true that "hanging" curve balls can be deadly for a pitcher, it's equally true that pitchers get beaten on pitches that do just what the pitcher wants them to do. Dizzy Trout, an outstanding pitcher for the Detroit Tigers, once said, "Every time somebody hits a home run off a breaking pitch, I hear somebody say that the curve ball hung. Unfortunately, it's not that simple. I've seen some real sharp breaking pitches wind up out there with the cash customers."

The knuckle ball is a pitch all its own. It acts like a butterfly in flight. Maybe a better description of the path of a knuckler can be found in the fact that Minnie Minoso used to describe an airplane that had been through turbulence by saying, "We had one of those knuckle-ball flights."

The knuckle ball has the big plus of being a difficult pitch to hit. It has the equally big minus of being a difficult pitch to catch. For that reason, it is a pitch to throw when there are no runners on base.

A comparison of best pitches is difficult. To say whether Walter Johnson or Sandy Koufax or Bob Feller or Sam McDowell was the fastest is impossible not only because of the difference in eras, but also because of the fact that any differences have to be marginal. Shortly after World War II, Feller was clocked with technical equipment belonging to the armed forces. The machines reported Feller's fast ball at 98.6 miles per hour. From

a distance of sixty feet six inches, it's doubtful that another mph or two would make much difference.

Comparing other pitches is also very difficult. About the only pitch in which there is a solid basis for comparison is the knuckle ball and most major-league hitters agree that Hoyt Wilhelm had the best knuckler they ever batted against.

Delivery is a study in contrasts. Some pitchers throw with an overhand motion, some three-quarters, some sidearm and some, as in the case of Ted Abernathy, "submarine" style. Some pitchers have motions that are easy to follow, while others' motions are terribly deceptive. Some are smooth, some are herky-jerky.

One of the most unusual belonged to Cincinnati pitcher Ewell Blackwell, who stepped toward the third-base foul line and threw with a sweeping sidearm motion. He was once described as looking not so much like a man pitching a baseball as like a man falling out of a tree. If you look at Blackwell's lifetime statistics, they are good but not sensational. Yet almost to a man every right-handed hitter who ever batted against Blackwell said he was the pitcher they least liked to face.

Certain pitchers find particular hitters troublesome. They will, if the situation allows, resort to what they call "pitching around" that hitter. Basically the philosophy is to give the batter only pitches that he doesn't like. If he swings, chances are that it won't be a good swing. If the batter is walked—well, that's a possibility that the pitcher has already accepted.

There are pitchers who will tell you that they are better against the better hitters. They bear down harder than they do against the man who bats seventh or eighth. On the other hand, some pitchers will tell you that they dedicate themselves to getting out the weak hitters. Their premise is that the good hitter is going to get to you sooner or later, but the weak hitter shouldn't. Hence, make sure the weaker hitter doesn't get to you. (On the strategy involved in working against top hitters, perhaps the most revealing insight comes from former Red Sox' pitcher Frank Sullivan. Someone asked him how he pitched to Mickey Mantle. Said Sullivan, "With tears in my eyes.")

If pitchers are indeed a breed apart, then the relief pitcher is a breed apart even from other pitchers.

Relief pitchers are evaluated on the basis of talent and stamina, never on their reaction to tough spots. Relief pitchers accept the fact that they're not called on unless their team is in trouble. They also live with the fact that they have no idea when they leave for the ball park whether or not they'll get in the game. They might warm up every day for a week and never get a call. Still, they have to be ready. Their job is a tough one, an important one, and in recent years a realization of that fact has led to some interesting changes in the lives of relief pitchers.

For one thing, they are better paid. Also, while the

bullpen was once an area reserved for older pitchers who were no longer able to be starters, you now see young pitchers who reach the major leagues as relievers and spend their careers there.

While there have been some relief pitchers who have depended on the fast ball, the majority of them are breaking-ball pitchers. If they are brought into the game with men on base, they try to force the batter into hitting a ground ball. Ground balls lead to double plays. Most sinker-ball pitchers seem to be relievers for that reason. Good examples are Clem Labine of the Brooklyn Dodgers and, more recently, Jack Aker or Frank Linzy.

For the relief pitcher—and the starter, too—baseball's rule on substitutions works against them. While other sports may have players who excel in a particular situation, such players are a luxury in baseball. According to the rules, a player may be used only once in a game. A good example is Steve Hamilton. Hamilton's strong suit is getting out a left-handed hitter in a tough situation. Often he is brought in to pitch to one hitter. But should the situation arise again later in the game, Hamilton is no longer available.

The pitcher's job, whether he is a starter or a reliever, is a pressure job. Most people realize that. What is often overlooked is the complexity of the job. It was summed up once by the New York Mets' pitching coach, Rube Walker: "Pitching is the single most complex job in all sports. I've heard about the problems football players have learning books crammed with plays, but I still think pitching is more complex.

"Let's take a hypothetical situation: You're the pitcher, there's a runner on first base and nobody out. It's the seventh inning of a close ball game. You've got a few things to work out in your mind before you turn that ball loose: What kind of hitter is this guy? What's he looking for? What's my best pitch today? (Pitchers often find their fast ball is the most effective one game, and the curve ball the next.) How did I get him out last time? What is he trying to do? (Some hitters might be trying to hit the ball out of the park, while others might be trying to hit it behind the runner, and there's always the chance he'll try a bunt.) What's the runner on first doing? Will he try to steal? Is my defense lined up the way I want?

"When you've run all that information through your brain, you're ready to turn the job over to your arm. All you have to do is throw a baseball sixty feet six inches, and have it pass the batter just at the right place. A difference of a few inches could be the difference between a strike and a ball hit out of the park.

Oriole reliever Dick Hall in grimace delivery.

"Finally you throw it. It doesn't matter whether it's a home run, an out, a ball or a strike; you're now faced with a brand-new situation. This goes on for nine innings, and can happen against eleven different sets of players. You have to know the weaknesses and strengths of about two hundred and seventy-five different hitters, and you have to be ready to adapt to a hundred different situations against each of them."

Walker, incidentally, is an example of a trend toward selecting pitching coaches from the ranks of ex-catchers, rather than ex-pitchers. Like most baseball theories, it has its devotees and its dissenters. Those who believe in the theory claim that pitchers, during their active careers, are concerned only with their own particular style and ability. Catchers, on the other hand, are used to working with a variety of pitchers and pitching approaches.

The relationships between catchers and pitchers vary. Sometimes a pitcher will work so well and so closely with one catcher that he will want that catcher to work each time he pitches. More often, however, a pitcher learns to work with different receivers. A pitcher is most often motivated by a catcher's ability to hit—the same consideration that colors his evaluation of other teammates. Pitchers want to have in the lineup players who are most apt to build runs. A man who pitches a shutout doesn't get a victory unless his own team can score. Pitchers are not usually heard to talk about a catcher as being "a good handler of pitchers." By the same token, catchers aren't heard to use the description either. Managers are apt to use it, but it's likely that the phrase was best described by catcher Joe Garagiola who said, "A good handler of pitchers is a catcher who hits .300."

Pitchers and catchers work more closely together than any other pair of players in a team sport. The two are involved in every pitch, and before that pitch is thrown it is essential that they are agreed on the type and placement of that pitch.

The most immediate job of a catcher, when a game starts, is to determine what his pitcher's most effective pitch on this particular day will be. As Rube Walker mentioned, it is variable. Unless the catcher can determine where his pitcher will be most difficult to hit, the pitcher may not be in the game long enough to correct the mistake himself. Catchers learn that they must make this decision themselves because the pitcher's pregame warm-up can be either very misleading or very accurate. The man who has a good curve ball warming up may find that it deserts him when the game starts.

There are other areas in which the two must work closely. Take the case of the pitcher who continues to shake off the catcher's sign. Obviously, somebody's got to give. In most cases, the pitcher is going to win those arguments. He is the one who has to throw the ball, and to make a pitch effectively he must believe in it. If he is

195

Familiar scenes: Left, catcher in crouch, as seen through umpire's legs; above, a ball is fouled off, the catcher reaches for a new one.

forced to throw something he doesn't want to throw, he not only may do it ineffectively, but he has been provided with an alibi in case the ball winds up as a souvenir for somebody in the bleachers.

While batters can often create sticky situations between pitchers and catchers, it's the base runner who can really get them feeling uncomfortable with each other. Catchers feel that while they may look bad if a base is stolen, it is really the pitcher's responsibility to protect against it by keeping the runner close to the base. Pitchers, on the other hand, feel a resentment against certain catchers in a spot where a runner might be stealing. The pitcher feels that he wants to throw the batter a breaking ball, but the catcher asks for a fast ball. The catcher's chances of throwing out the runner are better if the pitcher throws a pitch that gets to the plate quickly. When situations like this develop, opposing players are sometimes treated to watching the pitcher and catcher conduct their own little war of nerves.

But for the most part a catcher is dedicated to the proposition that making his pitcher mad is not helpful. Sometimes, in certain situations, when a catcher thinks the pitcher is relaxing, for example, he might try to steam him up just to get the adrenalin flowing. But catchers, and everyone else in baseball, recognize that the pitcher who loses his temper also stands an excellent chance of getting into trouble. Mr. Rickey pointed that up often, saying that anger was more of an opponent to a pitcher than an opposing batter was. "Pitchers who lose control of themselves also lose control of the ball."

The use of psychology by the catcher is not limited to the pitcher he is working with. It is also employed against the batter he is working against. A catcher hopes to get the batter's thought processes confused. If he can do that, he has helped his team. It might be a word, it might be an action—it doesn't matter.

One of the most successful of these ploys was used by Birdie Tebbetts on several occasions. He would say to the batter, "I'm going to call for a fast ball. Get ready." That's all. While the batter was trying to figure out whether Birdie was telling the truth or trying to trap him, he wasn't concentrating on what he was up there to do.

The catcher's job, like that of the pitcher, looks easier than it is. To the non-baseball fan, it seems as though he does nothing more than catch the ball from the pitcher and throw it back. But look at a hypothetical situation. Seventh inning. Game tied, nobody out, a man on second base. The pitcher throws a fast ball. It's inside, and the batter takes it for a ball.

Now the catcher starts on his list of problems: How was that last fast ball? Is the pitcher starting to lose some of his speed? What is this hitter up here to do—that is, is there a bunt possibility or is he swinging away? What about the lead the runner is taking? Is there a possibility of throwing behind that runner? Is the defense lined up the way it should be? What does the pitcher want to

throw? What do I think he ought to throw? All these questions must be asked, answered and evaluated in the space of time between pitches. And after the pitch is thrown, a whole new set of problems has to be considered.

The partnership between catcher and pitcher has an effect in the area known as "brushing back the hitter." There are a number of theories on the purpose of such a pitch, and on its effectiveness. One thing is certain. Pitchers who depend on intimidating hitters don't enjoy longevity in the major leagues. In the first place, the easily intimidated hitter doesn't make it to the major leagues. In the second place, players know that if their team has a pitcher who is a "headhunter," retaliation will be swift.

Look at it, however, from the standpoint of the battery mates. The batter is a pronounced pull hitter, with power. Consequently the strategy is to pitch him outside, so he can't pull the ball. Ball one, outside. Ball two, outside. Strike one, on the outside corner. Now, the catcher notices the batter edging toward the plate, so he can lean over for that wide pitch. There are really only two alternatives. Both involve requesting the batter to move back. One way is to ask politely. The other is to let a high inside pitch do the talking. Only one of these methods has ever been known to work.

While pitchers usually don't have a preference in catchers, the reverse is not necessarily true. Certain types of pitchers are much harder for catchers to work with. Catching a pitcher who is wild is both mentally and

physically exhausting. Fast-ball pitchers, contrary to what a lot of people might think, are a lot easier on the hands of a catcher than a sinker-ball or curve-ball pitcher. Breaking pitches are generally "heavy" balls to catch, while fast balls seem to hit the glove more softly. As Roy Campanella once described it, "Catching Don Newcombe is like catching baseballs filled with feathers. Clem Labine, on the other hand, is like catching a shot-putter's toss."

The jobs of both the catcher and the pitcher were summed up best by Yogi Berra, who once said, "We work harder than anybody else on the team, but we also have more fun. And when we win, what a feeling!"

Tom Egan can't hold onto ball as Jackson brings home a run.

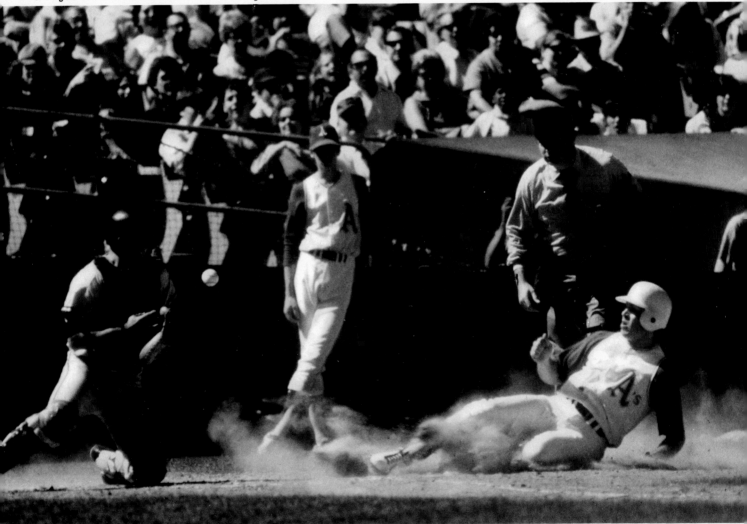

George Scott barrels in ahead of the play.

More than just speed

baserunning

by Milton Gross

Milton Gross has been a sports columnist for the *New York Post* since 1937. An MA from Columbia, Mr. Gross is the author of over 1,000 national magazine pieces and the author of three books, *Yankee Doodles, 18 Holes in My Head* and *Victory over Myself* (with Floyd Patterson).

Ray Fosse, the American League's All-Star catcher, moved a stride up from home plate toward third base and straddled the base line. He didn't know what was coming, just who—Pete Rose—and Pete didn't get his nickname Charley Hustle as a pacifist when running the bases.

Pete was running the winning run home in the bottom of the twelfth inning of Major League Baseball's forty-first annual All-Star game at Cincinnati's new Riverfront Stadium. He was racing a throw from center fielder Amos Otis of the Kansas City Royals following his own single, one by Billy Grabarkewitz of the Los Angeles Dodgers and one by Jim Hickman of the Chicago Cubs with two out. It came down to one of two things: a game-winning run to home or another extra inning. The throw to the plate apparently had Rose beaten.

Irresistible force versus immovable object, the

headfirst I could have had my neck broken. If I had slid in feet first, I could have had a leg broken.''

An All-Star game is an exhibition game; it is baseball's showcase, second only in attraction to the World Series, the season's singular opportunity for the nation's fans, in person and via countless millions of television sets, to see the best of one league pitted against the best of the other. The National League was going after its eighth straight victory, but even if it had been a preseason exhibition game at the Reds' Tampa, Florida, training base, Rose would have played it the same way. Some roses look prettier, some smell prettier, but this Rose has more thorns.

Like a ballcarrier in football going into the line and trying to open a hole where one had closed, Pete barreled into the catcher just as the ball arrived. The ball went off in one direction. Fosse's mitt flew from his hand and he was catapulted off his feet. Rose's

Robinson slides to third, starts to get up as ball gets away.

classic encounter. Fosse, the Cleveland Indians' 23-year-old rookie catcher, 6 feet 2 inches and 210 pounds of muscle and determination, was blocking the plate in the path of the hardest runner in the National League.

There were only three maneuvers the Cincinnati Reds' combative captain could make. He could slide feet first, attempting to finesse his way around Fosse to avoid a tag and touch the plate with his hand or foot through the back door. He could launch himself headfirst in a slide. Or he could attempt to bull his way through Fosse and bowl him over. These were the choices as Rose steamed the last half of the ninety feet between third and home.

"I was going to slide," said Pete, "and I saw I couldn't make it. Headfirst, it would have been worse. No way. I just had to run and hit him and hope to jar the ball loose if it had beaten me. If I had gone in there

momentum carried him toward the plate and he touched it with his palm for the run and the 5–4 National League victory.

"I never got hit like that before," said Fosse, who required hospitalization for a bruised shoulder following the massive collision.

"I just had to run and hit him. I got him with the knee, the whole body, everything, and he was crouched," said Pete, who wound up the game's hero. "I thought I had hit a mountain. It's like a guy in football waiting to tackle you—it's you or him. You see the end zone and you've got to go for the touchdown."

Maury Wills digs for first after chopping out a grounder.

"The boy had the plate completely blocked," said Gil Hodges, the Mets' manager and manager of the All-Stars that night. "Pete was going to score one way or another."

Which is precisely the point. Reduced to its simplest, the idea in baseball is to score more runs than your opponent and the only way to do it is to traverse the 360 feet from home plate to home plate. Each time a runner is able to advance an extra base by taking it or stealing it, by outlegging a throw on sheer speed or by a hit and run, or by taking advantage of a fielder's momentary mental lapse or error, he has reduced the distance by ninety feet and put more pressure on the defense.

The muscle way to score, of course, is by the home run, baseball's bomb. The cerebral way is by base-running, which must in no way be confused with pure speed. This is not the contradiction it may seem. Tommie Agee of the Mets, considered one of his team's most valuable players, for instance, is fast and a fairly decent base stealer, but he is not an exceptional base runner. His wheels, which are what ballplayers call legs, move swiftly in his peculiar rocking gait, but the wheels inside his head sometimes don't mesh with his physical movement.

The Mets failed to win the pennant in 1970. They might have, although Tom Seaver was something less than the perfect pitcher of the year before when the Mets won the World Series.

The night the Mets may have killed their last chance of overtaking the Pirates in the National League East came in the final series of the season between the teams. New York trailed Pittsburgh in the standings by two and a half lengths. With three to play, the Mets could have done it, but not when they failed to be opportunistic in their baserunning, while the Pirates capitalized on theirs.

The Mets went into the ninth inning of the Friday night game behind, 4–2. Ron Swoboda opened the inning with a walk. Agee belted a double off rookie John Lamb and became the tying run on second base with none out. In both dugouts you could almost smell the cerebration as managers Danny Murtaugh and Hodges had their tactics going on all burners.

The Pirates brought in lefty Joe Gibbon to pitch to left-handed-hitting Wayne Garrett. Hodges countered with right-handed-hitting Joe Foy. Foy walked on four pitches and up came Cleon Jones, who had been ordered to do one thing: Get Agee to third. Jones tried to bunt the runner over. He could not and on a 3–2 count the bunt sign was removed and Jones was ordered to swing away. He lofted a long fly to Roberto Clemente in right, which might have gone for extra bases, if the Pittsburgh right fielder had not gloved the ball near the wall. The runner could have moved to third, only Agee did not. He had come halfway down the line and with

Clockwise from above: Classic triad at second base—umpire, shortstop, runner; Pete Rose rises after headlong slide into second; Frank Howard, out at second, turns to glare at finish of play; Tommy Harper rounds third, dashes home.

the catch had to hurry back to tag up. By then it was too late to take the extra base on a sacrifice fly.

"I don't play safety-first baseball," said Agee. "When the ball was hit, I was sure it would be extra bases. I just wanted to get the tying run home. If I didn't think it was a base hit, I would have tagged up."

"Any time a man is on second with none out and his team is a run behind," said Hodges, in the game's postmortem, "he's got to tag up and go to third."

It was plainly not the best baserunning. Agee then attempted to atone for his original mistake. With one out and Art Shamsky at bat, Agee tried to steal third. On the attempt, however, Shamsky fouled off the pitch. With the count 2–2 on the batter, Agee again went for third. Shamsky tried to protect the runner with a half-checked swing. Catcher Manny Sanguillen threw

a perfect peg to Richie Hebner, guarding third base. Hebner applied the tag for the final out of the game.

"He," said Hodges, meaning Agee, "went on his own."

In that same game, Ken Boswell had been thrown out at the plate on Bud Harrelson's eighth-inning short single to left when coach Eddie Yost at third gambled on left fielder Willie Stargell not making the perfect throw. Stargell did. In the fourth inning, Sanguillen sent a drive into right-center, which Shamsky fielded, but the Pirates' catcher gambled and won when he stretched a double into a triple, putting Shamsky, who did not get to the ball quickly, to the test. Shamsky's

Below: Robinson heads for second. Danny Thompson is drawn off base, but Brooks makes the safe slide anyway. Right: Twins' Cesar Tovar attempts to upset Davey Johnson—unsuccessfully.

Runner at Oakland is a blur crossing first.

Top: Bobby Tolan loses helmet, but slides safely under gaze of unconcerned coach Kluzewski. Above: Don Buford waits at second, ready to break for third should throw be errant.

throw to cutoff man Ken Boswell was high and Boswell's relay was high. Sanguillen picked up the extra base and scored on Stargell's slow, high bounder to the right side of the infield.

"We win two in a row and we're still in good shape," Hodges said afterward.

Well, the Mets didn't. It wouldn't have been so necessary if the Mets had run the bases as they should have. "We just played bad baseball. They didn't," said Hodges, encapsulating perfectly a baseball basic. The pitcher throws, the batter swings. The fielder catches, the runner runs. Like all simplifications, this does not catch the complexities of a game that so intricately and inextricably combines the physical, the emotional and the cerebral.

Baseball has often been called "a game of inches," which is a cliché, but like all bromides, this description is based upon truth. It, in fact, explains the excitement and freshness baseball generates with each game. It is part war, without the killing, part chess, without the boredom. It is team against team, man against man, manager against manager.

What will Bobby Tolan do when he gets on first? What is Lou Brock going to do with his lead-off second? What will Maury Wills attempt at third? Do you pitch out, fearing a steal? Does the pitcher try a pick-off throw? Will the second baseman lean toward second base anticipating a steal attempt or a possible hit-and-run and thus find himself unable to cover his position if the ball is hit between first and the area he normally would be covering?

There are nine individual dramas being played out on the field at any one time and each demands something extra of each player. If a runner who would steal the pennies off a dead man's eyelids is on first base, the catcher wants a pitch high and on the outside, so he can throw quickly and nail the would-be burglar going down to second. Certainly he wants a fast ball. It gives the runner less of a time edge. But the pitcher may not want it. He may prefer to throw a curve or a pitch low and on the inside. The infielders, particularly the shortstop and second baseman, are tensing. One of them must cover. It is a duel of wits that sometimes breeds indecision. It has been estimated that a pitch takes only two fifths of a second to get from pitcher to catcher and few men stealing a base on speed alone could beat a ball thrown from the pitcher to the catcher and then to second base. But it is not speed alone. It is awareness. It is study. It is a sense of when to go and how much of a lead the runner can take on a pitcher.

Some pitchers have excellent motions to first base. Some do not. But no matter how effectively a pitcher can hold a runner on, he is going to be distracted from his main job, which is getting the hitter out. When a Tolan, who stole fifty-seven bases in 1970, or a Lou

Reggie Jackson scampers safely back to first on double-up play. Mike Epstein looks futilely to umpire for favorable call.

Brock, who stole fifty-one, or a Dagoberto Campaneris, who stole forty-two, is on base, he is making the pitcher more concerned with his taking a four- or five-foot lead off the base than with the man at the plate.

"A good deal of it is psychological," says Maury Wills, who set a major-league record with 104 stolen bases in 1962 and was caught in attempted steals that season only thirteen times. "That year, every time I got on, everybody expected me to go, not just the people in the stands. The pitchers did, the catchers did, the fielders did. Their anticipation can be both a help and a hindrance. But it just isn't all speed. It is studying the pitchers. You have to know the pitcher as well as yourself. You develop a sort of sixth sense about pitchers. Once I get on first I become a pitcher and catcher as well as a base runner. I am trying to think with them and know what they are going to do and in that way know what I am going to do. You've just got to apply yourself. A ballplayer with average speed can do it if he applies himself."

Base stealing is an art form that for the most part

lay dormant between 1915, when Ty Cobb stole ninety-six, and 1962, when Wills proved how valuable an adjunct to an attack swift feet and a wise head can be. Bobby Bonds of the Giants, who can hit with power, also is as adept on the bases as Willie Sutton was in banks. He stole forty-eight for the San Francisco Giants in 1970, besides hitting .302, which included twenty-six home runs and seventy-eight runs-batted-in. He can beat you with the bat; he can beat you on the bases—feats that generate the kind of excitement that Lou Brock of the Cardinals is also able to incite. Brock can hit. Brock can run. Brock can take the extra base. Brock, in short, is a one-man package of psychological warfare He can distract the opposition. He can lift up the Cardinals.

"I would rather have him hit a double than get on base with a single and then start jockeying around," manager Dick Williams of the Boston Red Sox was

quoted as saying after Brock almost completely disrupted his team in the opening game of the 1967 World Series, a Series that Brock turned into his private poaching preserve with twelve hits, seven stolen bases and several runs scored when he admittedly "cheated."

Brock opened the Series, which was eventually won by the Cardinals in seven games, by singling off pitcher José Santiago and immediately stealing second base. He closed it with a couple of hits and three stolen bases. In the first game his seventh-inning single and theft of second base led to the winning run. Twice he scored from third on infield outs by Roger Maris. "I was cheating more than halfway on those plays," said Lou. "I'll do that because I know the man will hit to the right side."

Nobody in Fenway Park had any doubt of Brock's nefarious intentions. In the city that still remembers the Brink's robbery, everybody had to anticipate Brock's robbery. Certainly Santiago knew what Lou intended to do. He threw to first base twice on Brock's second stolen base in the game and then pitched out, but Brock was off and running on the first pitch to the batter.

Preceding pages: Willie Smith of the Cubs slides home against the Giants' Dick Dietz. The call is "out" and Smith, to say the least, objects. Dietz raises glove to show ball.

The ball and Brock arrived simultaneously at second base, but the throw was eighteen inches off the ground. If it had been eight inches lower, Brock would not have made the steal. The fielder could have brought the glove down for the tag. This is the difference between success and failure on a steal.

There are, of course, others. "What I do," says Lou, "is come out early and watch a pitcher warming up. I watch his delivery and his motion and the time it takes him to release the ball. Every pitcher has a flaw. It's just a matter of observing it and appreciating how you can take advantage of it. They [the Red Sox] knew I was going to go on the first pitch, but so did I. If I could do it the first time, I had a psychological edge. What I try to do is create a situation in which the opposition

gets anxious. I don't believe I can be thrown out trying to steal second base if I get the proper jump on the pitcher. If they pitch out on me, 90 percent of the time I can anticipate the pitchout."

The Tigers could do as little with Brock the following year in the 1968 World Series, when Lou again stole seven bases to tie the Series mark he had set against the Red Sox. "What the hell, he's Speedy Bandido," said Mickey Lolich, a left-handed pitcher, which proves that if you learn your lessons in larceny well, your marks are not only right-handers, who have to peer over their left shoulders to watch the runner and keep him tied to the base. "He gets a good jump, he can outrun the ball. What can you do?"

Oddly enough the Tigers beat the Cardinals in seven games in the Series and it was Lolich who won three of them. He would never have gotten the opportunity, however, if Brock had slid into home plate instead of attempting to come in standing up.

Clockwise from top: Brooks Robinson can't escape tag of Tommy Helms; Richie Hebner from second to third; Tom Haller tries his best to deter Ron Hunt from completing play.

Early in the fifth game Lou was cut down on an attempted theft when Lolich did pitch out. Worse, with the Cardinals ahead in games three to one and ahead 3–2 in the fifth inning, Lou was on second when Julian Javier singled to left. He raced Willie Horton's throw to the plate and seemed to have it beaten, but was called out by umpire Doug Harvey.

"Harvey told me," said Tigers' catcher Bill Freehan, "that Lou would have been safe if he had slid. He just never touched the plate."

"If I had slid," said Brock, "he [Freehan] would have had a good chance of blocking me out. He was standing wide-legged, his feet three or four feet apart, one up the third-base line, the other at the corner of the plate. If you slide, he gets down on one knee and you don't get in. I had it beat all the way. I beat the ball to the plate, no doubt about it. It wasn't even close. I touched the center of the plate between Freehan's legs. When I hit Freehan, he went one way and I went another and that's when the umpire called me out."

"Why?" Brock asked Harvey.

"Because you didn't touch the plate," the ump answered.

"Why would Freehan come behind me and tag me if he had tagged me before?" Brock argued.

"The reason I tagged him a second time," said Bill, "was I saw him coming back, like a reflex, you know."

"The only time he did tag me," Brock persisted, "was when he came up behind me as I was arguing with the umpire."

"Frankly," Freehan said later, after the Tigers had overcome the Cardinals' 3–2 lead, won the game, 5–3, and gone on to win the Series, "it looked to me as though Lou came up short of the plate. I was surprised he didn't slide. There I was set, with my left foot planted where it was. He'd have had to slide through it or touch the plate with his hand simply because I was between him and the plate. When he hit me on the left side, he just spun away from the plate. I know it's going to be bang, bang, like that, because I'm watching the ball and see that it's a good throw."

Thus, for the want of a slide, a game and a World Series may have been lost by a player who tied the Series mark of thirteen hits for seven games and stole everything but the catcher's mask. It seems ironical, but it is true. To this day, Brock insists he was safe, but the record book still shows that the Tigers were world champions for that season.

Unfortunately, the record books do not carry any dark agate lines that reflect the ability of a base runner to see the entire kaleidoscopic potential of a play in front of him and the sixth sense to know how far he can capitalize upon it. Consequently we have runners who invariably know when they can go from first to third on a single. They seem to be able to change gear in stride, going into overdrive as they decide that an outfielder has not played a ball quickly enough. There are many. Hank Aaron of the Braves, for all of his age, is one. Willie Mays of the Giants is another. Frank Robinson of the Orioles is a third. Among the younger players, the Mets' Bud Harrelson is exceptionally adept and so is Tommy Harper of Milwaukee.

There are many others who immediately see the picture, are able to analyze it and distill the maximum from it. When such a runner is on base, the fielders hurry to make the play, sometimes committing errors in their anxiety to discourage the man from going. It is much the same way that infielders, feeling they must rush a play, try to throw the ball before they have actually fielded it and grasped it properly when a swift runner has hit a slow roller to the infield.

There is another element to baserunning, much more specialized, that can spread consternation among pitcher, catcher and third baseman. That is the peculiar talent to steal home. Not too many men have it. Not too many are given the office to try it, but somebody like Rod Carew of the Twins breeds terror when he gets on third base.

There is a line in the record book for that and next to Carew's name, it reads: Most times stealing home, season—7. That puts Rodney Cline Carew in with a very special person in a very special category. Pete Reiser of the old Brooklyn Dodgers accomplished that rare feat in 1946. That was a year after Carew had exhibited his first indication that he would be a young man in very much of a hurry. His mother, Olga, heavy with child, was aboard a railroad train on her way to a clinic in Gatun, Panama, to have her baby, but the baby wouldn't wait. He was born in the railroad car and was named after Rodney Cline, a doctor, a passenger on the train, who completed the delivery.

There may be nothing as satisfying or exhilarating or disrupting as the completion of a steal of home. It is never attempted on orders from the bench. The manager cannot know whether the pitcher will allow the runner to get the break or lead he needs. The best the runner will be advised is, "If you get a chance to try it and you think you can make it, then go."

It is best attempted, of course, when the batter hits from the right side. He blocks the view of the catcher, who can hear the footsteps of the runner pounding down the path if the crowd's roar does not drown them out. What made Carew's record-tying steal of home on July 16, 1969, so remarkable was that John Roseboro, who hits left-handed, was the batter.

The mere fact that Carew had already set the American League record with his sixth try just a month earlier made Chicago pitcher Jerry Nyman acutely aware that he would try it again. But being aware also left him somewhat uptight. Similarly, catcher Don Pavletich had to be prepared, knowing that Carew might break on him. Twice Rod feigned dashes for home. Twice he

It may seem easy. It is not. There are dangers. Unless the runner has signaled the batter that he is coming, he could be decapitated if the batter swings and pulls the ball down the base line directly into the path of the runner.

Ask Tommie Agee. He barely missed becoming a modern Ichabod Crane in the Mets' second National League play-off against Atlanta on October 5, 1969. Agee tried to steal home without warning his teammate and Mobile, Alabama, neighbor, Cleon Jones, who was at bat. Jones pulled the ball foul.

"The Mobile Express was almost derailed," said Manager Hodges.

"Cleon," said Agee, "you're trying to kill me."

Ty Cline scores winning run in play-off victory against Pirates.

retreated as Nyman, a southpaw, would not allow him to take too much of a running start. But Nyman finally had to pitch to Roseboro. The pitch was low and outside, perfect for avoiding any screening by the batter, but with a runner bearing down on him from one direction and a pitch coming from another, no catcher can maintain himself with the calm bearing of a squatting Buddha. The ball arrived with time to spare, but Pavelitch neglected to hold on to it. Eagerness or apprehension made him uncertain. Carew had seven for seven steals of home.

"Tommie," said Jones, "you're trying to mess me out of an RBI."

"Mess you?" said Agee. "That ball just missed my head. If it had hit me they'd be saying, 'There goes Tommie all over the place again.'"

"Man, you got me all upset," said Jones. "I hear you coming and I tried to miss the ball."

Which is what happens when one team runs another out of a ball game on the bases. Speed kills.

The incomprehensible art

hitting

by William Leggett

In twelve years at *Sports Illustrated* William Leggett has
advanced from reporter to senior editor. In that period he has
covered every major sport and for the past six years has been
that magazine's chief baseball writer. His only book, scheduled
for release in 1969, was never published.
Title: *The Cardinal Dynasty*.

y Cobb, because he held his hands apart on the handle of his bat, was said to swing at a baseball like a man working a broom. When Stan Musial dug himself in at home plate and looked out at the pitcher he was described as a guy peeking around a corner. Tony Oliva stands so far back in the batter's box he should be paid for moonlighting as an umpire, yet Sam Mele, a man who managed Oliva, once said of him, "Tony is such a fine hitter that he could hit .300 wearing boxing gloves."

How difficult is it to put a round bat on a round ball? A man can become wealthy enough to build condominiums in Bimini if he can consistently hit a ball safely only three out of every ten times at bat; if he is that rarity who fails only six times out of ten, people rush to build imposing statues in his honor.

Even among the best of hitters there is disagreement about technique, the relative advantages of various spots in the batting order, even the significance of the statistics themselves. Put three fine hitters together with a tape recorder and the playback will be a mélange of argument about eyesight and bat speed, concentration and fear, the breaking pitch and the in-and-out swing, guessing and waiting. The science of hitting is at best a thin one and very personal as well, and to those good enough to master it, it is the most financially rewarding aspect of professional baseball.

Who masters it, then, and how?

Written inside the protective batting helmet of Lou Brock, the St. Louis Cardinals' fine lead-off man, is the simple word HUSTLE. As a batting average of .391 in three World Series has shown, when Brock is playing up to his own definition of hustle he is among the most devastating performers in history. Although capable of tremendous home-run power, Brock's job is to get himself on base and thus ignite the St. Louis attack. When Brock is on his game he can produce more runs than a pair of panty-hose in a briar patch. His job as a lead-off hitter is to try to score 100 runs or more a season and collect 200 hits. Since 1964 Brock has averaged 104 runs and 193 hits, garnishing those figures with an average of 57 stolen bases a season.

Willie Stargell of the Pittsburgh Pirates is another hitter who keeps things under his cap, but Willie's ends and means are different from Brock's because Stargell hits in a different position in the batting order and is judged on his ability to drive in runs rather than score them. Each spring Willie writes a set of numbers into his headgear and then puts a piece of tape over them for reference during the course of the season. For Stargell, a good year is a .300 average, thirty homers and a hundred runs-batted-in. But Stargell as a hitter has less control over achieving his goals than Brock. When students of statistics run their fingers down the column headed RBI (runs-batted-in) and see that Willie hasn't produced the hundred, he is accused

Left: Hal Lanier strokes ball toward the night. Path of ball is made obvious with help of camera. Above: Newest thing in weighted bats is heavy rings of varying densities.

of failing. No records indicate whether his teammates successfully reached base ahead of him, giving him runners to knock in. Which man has the harder job, Brock or Stargell?

No matter what position a man hits in the batting order, there are pressures that can build up. In 1962, for example, Maury Wills of the Los Angeles Dodgers hit .299, stole a record 104 bases and became the National League's Most Valuable Player. Batting behind Wills was Jim Gilliam, a tremendous team player with an excellent eye and a superb judgment of the strike zone. Time and time again Gilliam fouled off pitches to protect Wills when he felt that Maury did not have a safe enough jump on the pitcher to steal successfully. Gilliam also swung at a lot of bad pitches to confuse the opposing catcher so that Maury could reach the next base. Hitting under these circumstances Gilliam

went up to the plate 702 times and struck out only 35 times—a remarkable job.

Hitters, nevertheless, are measured against .300. A man who compiles an average of .300 or over is regarded as a star. Most casual fans don't appreciate how small the gap is between a .280 hitter and a .300 hitter. Assuming that two men go to bat 600 times in a season, the .300 hitter will collect 180 hits while the .280 hitter will get 168. That figures out to only one more base hit every two weeks! A good hitter needs to be a little bit lucky, too.

The cliché says that "Good hitters are born and not made," yet recent seasons have produced several players who have worked hard enough at their trade to vault above their anticipated potential. Little Cesar Tovar of the Minnesota Twins is one of the best examples in the major leagues today of a man who dedicated himself to becoming a better batter and who did it

Opposite, clockwise from upper left: Bobby Bonds awaits blurred delivery from Ray Lamb to catcher Scrap Pile Stinson; Lee May doubles down the line; Frank Howard returns to dugout after striking out; Gerry Moses meets the ball on the nose. Above: Marty Keough crosses the plate in pain.

Clockwise from above: Reggie Smith goes down to stroke ball at knees; Jim Fregosi off on a hit; Roberto Clemente gets only a piece.

under very difficult circumstances. Tovar stands only 5 feet 9 inches and weighs 150 pounds. Because of the needs of his team he has played every infield and outfield position at one time or another and once even pitched an inning. (In 1968 he worked against the Oakland Athletics and got Bert Campaneris to foul out to third, struck out Reggie Jackson, walked Danny Cater and got Sal Bando to foul out.)

That spring Tovar had maintained that if he were allowed to play at only one position he could hit .280. Again shuffled around, he managed a respectable .272. "I try for two hits a game," Tovar says, "and pick up different bats all the time. When I hit the ball good but right at somebody I try not to get mad."

Tovar is a fascinating hitter to watch. He constantly fakes bunts to draw the infield out of position and his study of the opposing pitchers is intense. Because of his size and weight Tovar is not expected to hit many balls out of the parks, but in 1970 he hit ten homers and finished only two total bases behind Boog Powell, the American League's Most Valuable Player. Cesar also hit .300.

Just a few seasons back there were those who could foresee the day when the .300 hitter might disappear because pitching had become such a dominant force in baseball. But in 1969 the mound was lowered and the strike zone altered to help put more offense back into the game and the idea worked. Today there are those who believe that a man may again have a chance to hit .400 because of the use of artificial surfaces. Ted Williams, at .406 in 1941, was the last man to hit for that high an average and since then only Stan Musial's .376 in 1948 and Williams' .388 in 1957 genuinely approached .400. Williams was thirty-nine at the time and the oldest player ever to win a major-league batting title. Both Williams and Musial were tremendous students of hitting.

"It was the center of my heart, hitting a baseball," Ted has said. Red Schoendienst, Musial's road roommate for years, said, "He started to concentrate when he was tying his shoelaces in the clubhouse."

Williams and Musial had distinct advantages over the hitters of today. The players of the 1970s are constantly crossing time zones and play a majority of their games at night, when picking up the flight of a pitched ball is more difficult. The tendency to move relief specialists in and out of games is also much more common now than it was in the 1940s and 1950s. Proof of the differences between hitting in the daylight and at night is vividly demonstrated by some members of the St. Louis team that Schoendienst managed in

1966. Here is how some 1966 Cardinals hit at night and during the day:

Player	Night	Day
Lou Brock	.274	.301
Orlando Cepeda	.258	.373
Dal Maxvill	.230	.265
Tim McCarver	.269	.284
Mike Shannon	.259	.335

The increased use of relief pitching has become one of the major stumbling blocks for hitters. An examination of how the Boston Red Sox won their eight American League pennants points out dramatically how the reliever came into vogue. From 1903 to 1918 Boston won six times and pitchers averaged 108 complete games each winning season. (In 1904 Boston played 154 games and had 148 complete games, the all-time record.) Not until 1946 did Boston win again and it was accomplished with 79 complete games.

Horace Clarke lashes ball up the middle.

And one need go no further than the 1970 world champion Orioles to discover how tight games are in the big leagues. While Baltimore won the 1969 pennant by 19 games and the 1970 championship by 15, the team was involved in a total of 112 one-run games. Pressure on the hitter grows with each passing season.

Although Babe Ruth did more to popularize and stir the public's imagination than any other hitter, Ty Cobb remains the hitting marvel of the ages. Cobb left behind monumental records that will never be approached, much less broken. Consider, for instance, if Hank Aaron and Willie Mays, who both reached 3,000 hits in 1970, hoped to reach Cobb's record hit total of 4,191. Each would have to play ball every season through 1975 and *average* 200 hits a year. Aaron has not had a 200-hit season since 1963, Mays since 1958.

In Cobb's final season of 1928 he hit .323. His lifetime average of .367 seems forever safe. "The secret

226

When the Red Sox of 1967 reached their "Impossible Dream" pennant they got by with 41.

The modern hitter expects to face a relief pitcher of one kind or another virtually every day. "Managers today send pitchers out to the mound to throw as hard as they can for as long as they can," says Musial. "If the starter gets tired, another pitcher comes in and his job is to throw as hard as he can for as long as he can. While the hitters are getting tired, the pitchers are still fresh. Most of the time you never get a tired pitcher to hit against. It wasn't always that way. Where there used to be one or two real good relief pitchers in the majors now it seems like every club has them—long men and then key men to pitch the last two innings if the game is tight."

Top left: Willie Stargell tries to check his powerful swing.
Above: Pat Kelly follows through after connecting. Right:
Ball and bat of Bobby Bonds about to connect as Perez crouches.

of hitting," he once said, "is the stance at the plate, an open stance for pull hitting and a closed one for pushing the ball—just like golf. If you're a left-handed batter, never try to pull a left-handed pitcher."

Those who hold that the artificial infields and outfields of the 1970s will help someone achieve a .400 season may not be studying the problem closely enough. Rogers Hornsby, Cobb and George Sisler were the only hitters in modern-day baseball to hit .400 twice. Since 1900 only eight men ever hit .400 for a season. It is a very rigid barrier and any man who can accomplish it will become a national hero. Sisler hit .400 twice, Cobb and Hornsby three times each. Hornsby compiled the second-highest lifetime average ever, .358, and the highest season average, a remarkable .424 in 1924.

At the time he arrived in the majors from Class D, Hornsby was a crouch hitter, who choked up on the bat and stood close to the plate. Miller Huggins, Hornsby's first major-league manager, helped Hornsby abandon the crouch and moved his pupil down the bat handle and back from the plate. Eventually Hornsby stood farther back from the plate than good hitters are supposed to, but still he became one of the game's best batters.

Branch Rickey, one of Hornsby's early managers and a man never at a loss for words, once described his trials with "The Rajah" thus: "I have shown a forgiveness almost divine toward this player. Outside influences have him hypnotized. I have overlooked the unspeakable names he called me, and if he will get into uniform, the slate will be wiped clean." Hornsby loved to play the horses, but he avoided movies and would not look out of train windows because felt both might hinder his eyesight and bother his hitting. Lee Allen, the late historian at the Hall of Fame in Cooperstown, once wrote of Hornsby: "He was frank to the point of being cruel and as subtle as a belch."

When Hornsby hit that .424, the highest average of this century, Allen considered it such a marvelous accomplishment that he later researched Hornsby's season to show just how consistent a man must be to get .400. Here is how Hornsby hit against every opponent that year:

Boston	.480
New York	.436
Philadelphia	.427
Brooklyn	.424
Cincinnati	.411
Pittsburgh	.393
Chicago	.387

The current hitter with the highest batting average, based on 500 or more games played, is Rico Carty of the Atlanta Braves. Carty, with an average of .321 over six major-league seasons, gave .400 a fine chase in 1970 only to find it one of the most elusive goals imaginable. Rico hit .366 in 1970, the highest average since Williams' .388 in 1957 and Musial's .376 in 1948. Carty is a free swinger, a poor outfielder and a delight to the fans because of his laughter and outgoing manner toward the paying customers. Carty is known in opposing dugouts as a guy who "can hit the ball off his ear and murder it with two strikes on him."

Late in his fine season (1970), Carty went into one of those desperate slumps that drive good hitters up walls. "I asked what I was doing wrong, and people told me that I was lunging at the ball. My manager rested me during the second game of a doubleheader and I sit and think about hitting. I make up my mind to wait on the pitch, and I do it." The slump had pushed Carty into a 2-for-24 proposition and such things destroy a man's chances of getting to .400. (Early in the season Rico had also endured a 3-for-20 spell.) He came out of his late slump with a thirteen-game hitting streak at .556, but the light had followed the dark too late to achieve .400. His breakdown against the opposition follows:

Chicago	.550
Houston	.458
Pittsburgh	.455
San Francisco	.443
New York	.419
San Diego	.333
Philadelphia	.333
St. Louis	.318
Montreal	.317
Cincinnati	.292

Nobody has ever been able to understand why even the finest of hitters go into such devastating slumps. Managers are as woefully inconsistent about how to end a slump as the hitters are themselves. For every manager who believes that the best way to end it is to let the victim "hit his way of it" there is one who says, "Sit him down and let him think it out."

Carty refuses to take any batting practice at all when he is in the grip of a slump. "Cut batting practice," Rico says. "Lots of times you can overtime yourself by hitting too much. Don't pick up a bat until the game starts."

Confidence is probably the single most important factor in the makeup of a good hitter. Ask a player why he is in the middle of a hot streak and the same answer comes at you: "I feel more confident up there. The ball looks bigger to me. I feel I can hit a fast ball in a dark room." The slightest of slumps brings out any submerged lack of confidence in hitters. As Stan Musial says, "You should never let a slump last more than two or three days. If one goes two or three weeks it will wreck your

Clockwise from above: Bert Campaneris gets his weight into swing; Mays watches a sky ball; John Ellis extends himself.

whole season. Trying to pull every pitch instead of going to the opposite field is one of the reasons hitters get themselves into slumps. A hitter in a slump should try to go to the opposite field for a few days. Once the hits start falling in, he'll have his confidence back."

Wes Parker of the Los Angeles Dodgers might well be the perfect example of a player who suffered a lack of confidence in himself as a hitter and then found it and became one of the most unexpected and truly exciting batters in today's game. Bright, strikingly handsome, well read and an excellent bridge player, Parker was known for five years with the Dodgers as a player who carried a golden glove and an ineffective bat. His failure to hit made Parker an enigma.

Parker did not cost the Dodgers anything to sign. He called the office one day and said he would like to play for them. They agreed. In 1963 Parker played most of the season at Santa Barbara, where he hit .305, good enough to get himself promoted to Albuquerque, where he finished the last twenty-six games with an average of .350. Brought up to the big leagues, Parker was a so-so hitter.

Until 1969 Parker's lifetime batting average was .245, including two seasons when he hit .238 and .239. In 1969

Parker became a hitter. "I remember my first time at bat in the major leagues," he said in the spring of 1970. "Bob Sadowski was pitching for the Milwaukee Braves and he threw three pitches right by me. I walked those hundred miles back to the dugout, knowing how it feels to try to hit in the major leagues. It's an instant way to know fear and insecurity. You can play baseball in your own backyard from the time you are a kid and make all the fielding plays that the major-league players make: diving stops, long runs, leaping catches. But nobody ever walked into my yard who could throw a ball like Bob Gibson or Jim Maloney or Sandy Koufax. There is a mystique to hitting in the major leagues that both bothers and fascinates even major leaguers. Unless you experience going from being a bad hitter to becoming a respectable one you can never explain the difference."

During the 1968 season Parker resembled almost the pluperfect case of a man standing at home plate doing little with the bat in his hands. Luckily he hit .255 during the first half of the season, because the second half found him averaging .193. When he left the Dodgers' clubhouse at the end of the year he was down to .239.

In 1969 Parker jumped his average to .278 and looked confident in the batter's box for the first time. What made the difference? Psycho-Cybernetics! Parker took a course in San Diego in this philosophy of positive thinking developed by Dr. Maxwell Maltz. "It was for four days," Parker says, "and I really got sold on the concept. The idea of it is to drive the fear of failure from your mind.

That fear is the biggest thing an athlete has to battle against. A hitter has to fight the fear of failure more than any other performer."

With the help of Psycho-Cybernetics and batting coach Dixie Walker, Parker became an excellent hitter in 1969 and might easily have hit .300 if an appendectomy at mid-season hadn't slowed him down. His .278 was a pleasant thing for Los Angeles and the Dodgers would have gladly accepted a repeat in 1970. What they got instead was a .319 season and 111 runs batted in!

"Baseball can be fun when you go up to the plate feeling you are going to get a hit," Parker says. "Once you have confidence in yourself that you *can* hit, there is a world of difference in the way you feel toward the game."

Parker, of course, is a switch-hitter, giving him the plus of having the curve break into him at all times. The Dodgers' organization believes strongly in switch-hitting —manager Walt Alston has brought his grandson up to switch-hit—not only because of the advantage against the curve but also for the confusion it causes the opposing manager. Through the years, switch-hitting has not truly produced as many good averages as one might think. Although it is being used more in the 1970s than ever before, only Mickey Mantle so far has been able to generate enough power from both sides of the plate to bring headlines.

Pete Rose of the Cincinnati Reds is one of the few present-day switchers who has record-breaking potential.

Entering the 1971 season, Rose has put five years with two hundred or more hits behind him and he is also that man most pointed to as having the chance to climb up toward .400. With the full artificial surface to work against in 1971, Rose could well turn the new Riverfront Stadium in Cincinnati into a hitting festival. He can run and is known as a slash hitter capable of driving ground balls through the fast surface of the infield. Rose's attitude has now been helped by the fact that he made himself into the first so-called singles hitter to draw a $100,000 paycheck. Like all good hitters, Rose's style is his own and he lets nobody fool with it.

Just as Rose admires Ted Williams, Ted Williams admires Rose. They also disagree on the way to hit. Prior to an exhibition game in the spring of 1970, Williams and Rose met in Tampa. Rose had read Williams' book on hitting; Williams' admiration of Rose had developed from seeing him play on television and examining his statistics. "I had a heck of a talk with him," Rose said. "Boy, is he enthusiastic! He talked to me about hips and wrists and eyes, and he had me swing and then took my swing apart step by step. He backed me up against a wall and kept talking to me and taking my swing and breaking it down to a science. I finally said to him,

231

Carl Yastrzemski, Pete Rose, Tony Conigliaro, Matty Alou.

'Ted, damn, if I played for you and had to listen to all this stuff you'd make a .200 hitter out of me.' ''

Aside from Mantle, Rose and now Parker, the best of the switch-hitters through the years have been Beauty Bancroft, Max Carey, George Davis, Frank Frisch, Red Schoendienst, Ross Youngs, and the present group that includes Maury Wills of the Dodgers, Reggie Smith of the Red Sox, Roy White of the Yankees and Don Buford of the Orioles.

People still argue whether Babe Ruth's sixty home runs and Roger Maris' sixty-one are equal to Joe DiMaggio's fifty-six-game hitting streak. It's a marvelous argument and one that will never be settled. It depends on the point of view and the value you put on baseball's fascinating statistics. How good a hitter is Hank Aaron?

Roberto Clemente? Pete Rose? How great were Cobb, Hornsby, Musial, Sisler? What about Billy Grabarkewitz, Bobby Bonds, Cleon Jones? Where does Willie Mays stand? Tony Oliva? Carl Yastrzemski? Al Kaline?

Hitting is one of the few skills left to man that leave him free to do his own thing his own way.

On his fiftieth birthday, Stan Musial sat surrounded by his grandchildren and spoke for all hitters. "If I had worked harder at it," he said, "I could have been better—I know I could have."

Don't all of them?

232

Above: Pete Rose doesn't like the strike-three call. Right: Adolpho Phillips watches his hit. Far right: Henry Aaron in standard form.

233

Beware of Moe

humor

by Roy Blount, Jr.

Baseball is a funny game. For various reasons discussed here,
the sport's humor is unique and a touch whacky. Dizzy Dean, Lefty
Gomez, Babe Herman are three men whose escapades and remarks
have been told and retold. Less known but equally funny are such
modern players as Cesar Tovar, Chico Ruiz, Lefty Phillips, Rocky
Bridges and the incomparable Moe Drabowsky. Their stories,
remembrances of the past, of the Mets and Casey Stengel and
zany others are told here by Roy Blount.

Mr. Blount, from Decatur, Georgia, is a staff writer at *Sports
Illustrated,* where his chief assignments concern baseball. Before
coming to that magazine, he was a columnist for the editorial
page of the *Atlanta Journal.*

In 1970, the year he won the National League batting title, someone came up to the Braves' Rico Carty and asked him, "What time is it?"

"Now?" Carty wanted to know.

Baseball may not sound as funny as squash, donkey basketball or quoits, and it may not be as funny as it once was—when Casey Stengel was tipping his cap to let a real bird fly out and there was always a pitcher around named Pfeffer or The Only Nolan (there has been only one The Only Nolan—Edward Sylvester Nolan—1878–85, and there hasn't been a Pfeffer in baseball, at any position, since Jeff Pfeffer in 1924)—but it is still pretty funny.

For one thing, it still has Stengel. Although no longer in uniform, he is often on the field before game time in some capacity (at the 1969 World Series he revealed that he was on hand to represent "the foreign press") and he is always bedazzling at banquets. Just recently he arose before writers, players and executives and said, "The last banquet I was at, I spoke so long two of the Four Horsemen died at it."

People who have never heard Stengel in person may think that Stengelese is an invention of sportswriters, but it is not. It is genuine and breathtaking, in the style of a gifted three-year-old child making up hair-raising stories to himself at night in the tub. And now, having said that, I am not sure that I can quote enough sustained Stengelese to bear out that description. Just remember that

Stengel once said, before a Congressional committee, that the game would never be quite right in Japan because "they are trying to play baseball with little fingers over there." He acknowledged his selection as baseball's greatest living manager in 1969 by saying, "I want to thank all my players for giving me the honor of being what I was."

I did manage to take down the following stretch of Stengelian dialectic during a baseball writers' dinner: "He said make sure your

Frank Howard: odd moment.

boys out there look like men on the field, if you got to play dirty, play dirty clean, and that was when we didn't have three changes of uniform instead of one. He was the one got married with his glove on. He said, 'This glove has meant a lot to me, why shouldn't I get married in it?' And he was the first to make $1,500 a year. Oh and they threw overhand, sidearm, underhand, any way in those days. . . ."

The historical breadth of those observations is significant, I think. Baseball is funnier than other sports in part because everything in it takes place against a lush background of Americana. The players still wear

knickers, after all, although today they may be skintight knickers (in *Ball Four* Jim Bouton reveals that Phil Linz of the Yankees never knew why, but he thought he could run faster in tight pants). In the case of the Pittsburgh Pirates, they are even knit, stretch-pants knickers. The new Pirates' uniforms have been compared to "ski pants, only all over," and to long johns, only not so long. The pants have an elastic band, a drawstring and no fly, so that one Pirate predicts that games will be held up because of a Pirate's having difficulty between innings. "It's like taking off a girdle," says Steve Blass.

But they are still knickers, and no ballplayer in uniform is ever entirely unevocative of the old pictures of Honus Wagner, standing in all dignity with his trousers billowing around his knees. The Presidency would be as funny as baseball if people pictured Calvin Coolidge in a tight collar standing just behind Richard Nixon every time the latter came into view.

The point I'm trying to make is that historical background helps make baseball funnier than, say, the pole vault. This background is evoked, often irrationally, whenever one of the myriad statistical records with which baseball is obsessed is broken or tied. I was walking down the hall at *Sports Illustrated* late one evening and heard Herm Weiskopf, a fellow baseball staffer, laughing softly in the cubbyhole where the AP news tickers are kept. "Looky here," Weiskopf called gleefully.

What had happened was that Cesar Gutierrez had collected seven hits in a single game. That was funny in part because Gutierrez had gone into the game with an average of something like .217, reflecting seven hits perhaps over the last

Catcher Romano and pitcher Buzhardt.

couple of weeks. It was funny in part because the seven hits had all been either grounders off somebody's glove or little bitty squibs or bloopers with eyes. The latter had no doubt dropped in "like dying quail." "Like a dying quail" is a baseball phrase, one of hundreds that are somehow funnier than those evolving from other sports. Baseball also has more flukes—pleasanter flukes—than other sports. What fluke is there in any other sport so droll as a "Chinese home run," for instance? Luck is funnier in baseball than in other sports—Gutierrez' good fortune calls to mind Bobo Holloman's no-hitter. In 1951 Holloman talked the St. Louis Browns authorities (and if the phrase "St. Louis Browns authorities" isn't funny to you, then you don't know baseball history) into letting him have one start before he was sent

down to the minors. Bill Veeck, the Browns' owner, had used a midget, Eddie Gaedel, to draw a walk in 1951. So Holloman got his chance, and in the first big-league start of his life gave up twenty-seven towering drives, blistering shots and blue darters, all of which were caught. Bobo Holloman went down in history as the only man ever to pitch a no-hitter in his first start. It turned out to be the only complete-game start he ever pitched.

But the main thing that night at the AP ticker was that the image of Cesar Gutierrez could be super-imposed on the image of another player of another time—that of Wilbert Robinson, and that, to me, is humor in baseball. For Gutierrez had tied the all-time major-league record for hits in one game, set some sixty years before by that gentleman, rotund even in his playing days with the old Baltimore Orioles. Robinson had established his everlasting reputation as the manager of the "Daffiness Boys" Brooklyn Dodgers of the late 1920s. He became known as "Uncle Robbie," a fat man in small round spectacles, forever shaking his head over some incredibility committed on the field by his players. Uncle Robbie was the manager of Babe Herman, a skinny, prominent-toothed farm boy, whose hat in pictures is always slightly skewed and too small, and who was famous for getting hit on the head by fly balls.

Actually, Herman claimed he had never been hit on the head by a fly ball. He even offered to retire from baseball permanently and to pay sportswriter Tom Meany $5 if he had ever been hit on the head by a fly ball. "How about on the shoulder?" Meany asked him.

"Oh no," said Herman. "On the shoulder don't count."

It was Uncle Robbie who once refused to have anything to do with Herman's small son, who was accustomed to climbing up on the manager's lap to get a piece of

candy. When the Herman nipper asked Uncle Robbie why the cold shoulder, Uncle Robbie said, "Go ask your old man why he ain't hittin'." Uncle Robbie was watching when, largely because of inspired baserunning by Herman, the Dodgers wound up with three men standing on third at the same time—and when, at least according to legend, Herman on steaming into second base passed a teammate steaming back to first.

Speaking of bad fielding and baserunning, surely ineptitude is funnier in baseball than in other sports. Bad defense in football or basketball is tragic, shameful, dismal. In baseball it is Dick Stuart earning the nicknames "Dr. Strangeglove," "Stonefinger" or "Ancient Mariner" (who stoppeth one in three). It is Curt Blefary

Score gives Zimmerman a headache.

becoming known as "Clank," and Ray Jablonski and Lou "The Mad Russian" Novikoff winning a warm spot in every heart because they persisted, without letting it weaken their characters, in being so awful afield. If a man has a good heart and can hit, bad fielding, at least in retrospect and at a safe distance, can come to seem almost a sign of grace, like a bear's inability to reason.

As for offense, it may be complicated in football, but it is complicated like the Federal

touching second on the way, as prescribed. The opposing manager, Baltimore's Earl Weaver, came out to protest, and time was called. Tovar, standing on first, was told by the Orioles' Boog Powell that he hadn't touched second. So Tovar ran over and slid into that base. Then, tired of all the embarrassment and hassle, he got up and went to the dugout. Rich Reese told him to go back to first, but Tovar said, "No way." Baltimore threw to first and Tovar was out on a five-minute double play.

runner from first and the throw from the outfield arrived there. Lefty took a quick look, gave out a terrible yell and joined them all with a slide from the coaching box.

Of course no discussion of complex fielding and baserunning can be closed without some mention of the pre-1969 New York Mets. (Just as no discussion of disappointing hitting should omit a reference to the 1968–69 California Angels, who inspired the remark, "They're like a box of Kleenex— they pop up one at a time.")

Dodgers—cooling off or just embarrassed?

238

budget is. Baseball offense is often complicated like a Marx brothers movie. Cesar Tovar of the Minnesota Twins is a player of unquestioned competence, but once in 1970 he took off from first on the hit-and-run and was past second when Rod Carew's fly to center was caught. Tovar raced back to first in time to beat the throw, but without

The Dodgers were not the only team ever to have three men on third. Lefty Gomez, the old Yankee pitcher, who stands with Herman among the game's all-time great screwballs, as they call them, once managed Binghamton in the Eastern League. He was coaching at third base one day, with men on first and second, when the batter singled to center. The runner from second sprinted around third, paused and turned to see if he had missed a signal to hold up. Playing it safe, he slid back into third just as the

Everybody has heard about the pre-1969 Mets. How Felix Mantilla would break the wrong way on ground balls. How Hot Rod Kanehl, at shortstop, once turned with the crack of the bat, flipped down his sunglasses, churned his legs and raced into left field in pursuit of a pop fly that Mantilla, playing third, caught right next to the pitcher's mound. How Marvelous Marv Throneberry kept failing to touch bases, like a man avoiding cow paddies or mines. For me the incredibility of the championship-winning Mets in 1969 was encapsulated, not in the kiss I saw a long-haired youth give a huge Irish cop on the field after the final game (the cop blushed), but in the diving catch Ron Swoboda made off Brooks Robinson's drive to right-center with two men on in the ninth inning of the fourth game. It was as great a catch as ever was made, even if, or even more so if, you agree with Frank Robinson that it was a bonehead play, that Swoboda should have cut the ball off on the hop. It was so great because Swoboda was such a representative Met—a Met of whom manager Gil Hodges has said, "He doesn't have coordination as we know it in baseball." Swoboda caught the ball one eighth of an inch off the ground, with his body extended absolutely fully. It was exactly as W. C. Fields used to do at dinner parties—drop someone's plateful of food, as a comedian might be expected to do, and then heart-stoppingly catch it, not a bean of it spilled, one eighth of an inch off the floor.

There were giants in the old days, to be sure, before there was anything much to be superimposed upon. Herman "Germany" Schaefer, who knocked around in the majors from 1901 to 1918, once announced to a hostile crowd in Chicago that they were about to witness an exhibition by "the world's greatest hitter." As they hooted and jeered, Schaefer took two strikes and then hit one out of the park. As he touched first, he yelled, "Schaefer is into first!" He threw a hook slide into second and shouted, "Schaefer beats the throw!" He slid headfirst into third and cried, "Schaefer safe by a mile!" He sprinted toward the plate and crossed in, barreling

through a cloud of dust. "Ladies and Gentlemen," he cried, upon arising and brushing himself off, "Mr. Herman Schaefer, the world's greatest hitter, thanks you for your kind attention." He also played a whole inning at second base in a long raincoat, trying to convince an umpire to call a game. And once, with a man on third, he stole second, and when that didn't draw a throw, he stole first right back on the next pitch. That didn't draw a throw either, but it made Germany Schaefer immortal.

Rube Waddell, a great left-hander for Connie Mack's turn-of-the-century Philadelphia Athletics—who looks a little bit like Red Skelton—was best known for going off somewhere and getting drunk or going fishing or falling in with a marching band or joining a sandlot game on the day he was supposed to be pitching. It is said that he originated, by acting it out, the joke about the drunk who decided one night that he could fly, and in order to convince some doubters, jumped out of his hotel window flapping his arms. When Waddell awoke in the hospital, he asked his roommate what he had done. When his roommate told him, he cried, "I coulda been killed! Why didn't you stop me?"

"What?" Waddell's roommate replied. "And lose the hundred bucks I had bet on you?"

It adds a great deal to this anecdote to know that Waddell's roommate was named Ossee Schreckengost and that Schrecken-gost (where are all those great old German baseball names? Angel Bravo and Cesar Geronimo and Rollie Fingers are pretty good, but where are the Boots Poffenbergers today?) stuffed his mitt with ostrich feathers in order to handle Waddell's fast one, and that Waddell once went to Connie Mack and demanded a new contract requiring Schreckengost to stop eating crackers in bed.

Babe Herman, the player who

hedged on fly balls off his shoulder, also once beseeched a sportswriter to think of Herman's family, his reputation, and stop portraying him as a clown. The sportswriter agreed that Herman had a point, until Herman pulled a lit cigar out of his pocket and walked off puffing it.

Dizzy Dean and some of his fellow Gashouse Gang St. Louis Cardinals once dressed up in painters' clothes and repainted half of one wall of the lobby of the hotel where they were staying. Later, as is well known, Dean got into television work, broadcasting games of the week and saying "slood" (to rhyme with "stood," not "slud," as Dean's noted past tense of slide is invariably spelled), "throwed," "prespiration" and "the players have returned to their respectable positions." He was also adept at singing "The Wabash Cannonball" and hollering down from the TV booth to people on the field, who sometimes waved back.

Lefty "Goofy" Gomez was the first pitcher to give credit to "clean living and a fast outfield," and it was he who struck a match at home plate one overcast day to make sure a terrifyingly fast Bob Feller could see not to hit him. Gomez once paused in his mound work to watch an airplane go by overhead. When shortstop Tony Lazzeri came in from his position to complain, Gomez said, "You take care of shortstop and spaghetti, and I'll take care of airplanes and pitching."

Yogi Berra is not as funny a person as he has been made out to be, but he did once complain to a manager that he couldn't think and hit at the same time, and he was a funny outfielder in his last couple of years with the Yankees. I once saw him catch a routine fly ball so off-balance in left field that it knocked him down, and he stayed down long enough for not only the runner at third, but also the runner

239

at second to tag up and score.

I once saw Rocky Bridges, coach of the Angels, pick up pitcher Andy Messersmith's glove from the bench, spit it full of tobacco juice and put it back down, and I still say he is a funny coach. In the minor leagues he once gave a signal from the third-base coaching box while standing on his head, and another time, in a tense situation, a hitter looked down to Bridges for a sign and saw him standing there sticking his tongue out at him. Bridges once broke his jaw; he complained that "the trouble with having your jaw wired is that you can never tell when you're sleepy—you can't yawn."

During the year Bridges was managing the San Jose Bees in the California League, he said: "In one game, there is a man on first, one out and my pitcher is up. 'If you don't bunt him over on the first pitch,' I tell him, 'hit and run on the second.' He misses the bunt, takes the next pitch and the guy's thrown out. 'How can you blow a sign when I told it to you?' I ask him. 'Well,' he says, 'I forgot.' Four days later there's a man on first, one out and my pitcher is up. Different pitcher. 'If you don't bunt him over on the first pitch,' I tell him, 'hit and run on the second.' He misses the bunt, takes the next pitch and the guy's thrown out. 'How can you blow a sign when I told it to you?' I ask him. 'Well,' he says, 'I forgot.' For the life of me," said Bridges, "I couldn't see how they could do it twice in one week."

Bridges' immediate supervisor on the Angels is Harold "Lefty" Phillips, the team's manager, who is widely considered to look funny. "Lefty doesn't care about his pants,"

240

Sonny Jackson gets assist.

says Angels' general manager Dick Walsh. "As long as they stay on around the waist, he doesn't think about what they look like." And anything that fits Lefty's waist is likely to have no relation to the rest of his body. As a manager his pot is somewhat reduced and his pants somewhat more nearly snug overall than they were when he was a coach, but he still looks as though he might be keeping a few extra infield balls in his trouser legs (we were speaking of knickers earlier) and maybe an extra infielder under his belt. "Lefty looks like the least likely baseball man," says Sandy Koufax, "but you have

Tito Fuentes in not-uncommon stance.

to listen to him, you can't just look at him."

Listening to him, you are reminded that baseball is one of the last enterprises left that still provide men who pronounce everything through a mouthful of either chewing tobacco or chewed cigar, as Lefty does. And he says remarkable things, such as, "I'm planning my pitching rotation out through the All-Star break for the sake of the armed forces," which means not that he is trying to give the Defense Department some kind of break but that he is allowing for the days his pitcher will miss for reserve duty. A recent Phillips conversation of some interest went on between him and a Baltimore scribe who complained about the attitude of Alex Johnson, the Angels' outfielder, who once dumped coffee grounds into an offending typewriter.

"Didn't he talk to you?" asked Lefty, grinning.

"Yeah, but I wasn't sure I was going to live through it," said the writer.

"You mean verbally?" asked Lefty.

The Angels also have Chico Ruiz. Ruiz prides himself on being baseball's premier bench warmer, and he has a special cushion and special alligator shoes for use in that role. The last official act of Ruiz as a National Leaguer was to wrap himself in a blanket, tie a feather to his head with a belt, stick a knife in his teeth and pounce on Chief Nok-a-Homa, mascot of the Atlanta Braves, as the Indian passed through the infield on his way to his left-field teepee.

Chief Nok-a-Homa sits out behind the left-field bullpen in Atlanta

Ex-roomies Javier and White exchange pleasantries.

Stadium in his teepee waiting to send up smoke signals and do a war dance whenever a Braves' player hits a home run. He is a real Indian, an Indian insurance salesman. At one point the Braves had a guy with a mustache out there. It was either that Chief Nok-a-Homa or the real Indian, the insurance man, who set fire to himself and the teepee once in the process of sending up signals.

"I thought he was an old guy," Ruiz recalls in relating the capture of Chief Nok-a-Homa. "But no, I have a hard time catching him and then he throws me up in the air. But I catch him again in the bullpen, two of our pitchers help me there and I pull hees blanket off what hees wearing and it's a good thing hees got on pants underneath 'cause *heeda been naked!*"

Someone else who is a lot of fun if you don't mind snakes is Moe Drabowsky, relief pitcher for the Orioles. Wherever the Orioles stop, Drabowsky finds a pet shop, buys some snakes and takes them to the clubhouse to throw them on Paul Blair, who minds them so much he can't stand it. Drabowsky also takes pride in his moving $50 bill gag. He takes a $50 bill, affixes a long black thread to it and plants it on the floor of a hotel lobby. Someone comes in, spies it

and casually moves to put his foot on it. Drabowsky then moves it just out of the foot's way. The person casually moves to put his foot on it again, and Drabowsky moves it again. In that way he has been known to pull a prosperous-looking conventioneer all the way across the lobby of a large hotel, in tiny little hops. Another time he had a little old lady down crawling on her hands and knees. And sometimes he will give the thread a jerk, causing the bill to fly in the air as though a gust of wind has come in through the door and caught it—so as to see what kind of things people will do to bat down a flying $50 bill. On a team that works very hard to give people hotfoots, Drabowsky works the hardest. He will leave a long track of lighter fluid—around a corner, between himself and the match in the victim's sole—so as to remain anonymous.

But not to history. It was Drabowsky who in 1966, having played for Kansas City earlier in his career, was aware that in the Kansas City ball park you could call the home bullpen from the

241

Manager Hodges: Grounds rules can be funny.

visitors' bullpen phone. So he rang up the Athletics' bullpen, imitated the voice of Kansas City manager Alvin Dark and said, "Get Krausse throwing." And to Dark's consternation the Kansas City bullpen coach did. The next day Drabowsky called again, imitated the voice of A's owner Charlie Finley and demanded an explanation of the whole matter.

When Drabowsky was traded from Baltimore back to Kansas City, he started a famous feud between the two bullpens, which entailed relief pitchers skulking back and forth beneath stands with paint for redecoration, cherry bombs, small rocks for bombardments and goldfish to leave swimming in the water cooler. During the 1969 World Series, before Drabowsky was traded *back* to the Orioles (humorists tend to move around a lot), he hired a plane to fly over the Baltimore ball park towing a sign that said "BEWARE OF MOE."

The bullpen, in fact, is one of the main things that keep conscious hilarity in baseball. There is plenty of time out there for thoughtful tomfoolery, such as stuffing Ralph Kiner's glove full of peanut shells and grass, as Joe Garagiola remembers someone doing. Another favorite activity in bullpens is choosing all-ugly teams, all-guys-you'd-most-hate-to-meet-in-a-street-fight teams, all-terrible-person teams and so on. Do other

Willie Mays: "Yours!"

sports have such a richness of material for such imaginary teams, or such leisure for players to imagine in? I think not. No other sport has anything quite like the all-time registers of players in baseball's various encyclopedias, either—a wealth of names like Joe Rabbitt, Noodles Hahn, Alamazoo Jennings, Orval Overall, Dell Conrad "Wienerwurst" Darling, Robert (get this) "Ach" Duliba and Hugh I. "One Arm" Daily. From such names you can come up with anything. An all-time fish team:

1B. Silas "Lefty" Herring (1899, 1904)
2B. Robert H. Sturgeon (1940–48)
3B. John E. Bass (1877)
SS. Chico Salmon (1964–present)
OF. George Silas "Gentleman George" Haddock (1888–94)
OF. Ralph Garr (1968–present)
OF. Jesse Willard Pike (1946)
OF. Turbot . . . . (1902)
C.   Edward C. Whiting (1882–86)
P.   Dizzy Trout (1939–52)
P.   Jim "Catfish" Hunter (1965–present)
P.   Norm Bass (1961–63)
P.   Paul "Lefty" Minner (1946–56)
P.   Bill "Smoke" Herring (1915)
P.   Arthur L. "Red" Herring (1929–47)

And too many other herrings to mention. And that's not even using Preacher Roe. "Turbot . . . ," by the way, is one of those mysteries that baseball's history is obscurely cataloged enough to embrace. That is the only way this individual is identified in the 1956 Official Encyclopedia of Baseball, which claims that he played one game for the Cardinals in 1902. He isn't identified at all in the latest encyclopedia, which was compiled by use of a computer. I don't know what happened to him, but we need him in the outfield.

Fritz Peterson, the Yankees' pitcher, is funny. He has dreams —that Tom and Nancy Seaver are sitting on the end of his bed, for

Reggie Jackson: decapitator?

instance—and tells reporters about them. Once during a five-game Yankee winning streak, Peterson said that manager Ralph Houk was so pleased "When we tied the score and I leaped up and put my finger in his eye, he just laughed."

Peterson's former teammate, Steve Hamilton, has a pitch he calls the Folly Floater. Hamilton stops his windup at the top and then tosses the ball like a man throwing a dart softly. It goes way up in the air and comes down in the strike zone maybe. During a 1970 game between the Yankees and the Indians, Tony Horton fouled one Floater off, called for another one, got it, popped it up and crawled back into the dugout on his knees.

Steve Blass of the Pirates, who bills himself quietly as "the only person ever to leave Falls Village, Conn.," will do things like tie his tie so that only a small tab of it is showing and then go into an airplane and tell the stewardess, "I'm the one with the short tie."

Billy Martin is better known as a fighter than as a rhetorician, but in 1970 he responded to an imagined insult from Earl Weaver by declaring, "Let me say, I could win with the Baltimore team under any condition: a salami and a pizza in my mouth, two big cheeses in my ears, blindfolded and not knowing the situation."

Bob Uecker, a former non-hitting catcher, who now helps telecast the Atlanta Braves' games, got a good deal of material for the banquet talks he gives when he was trying to catch Phil Niekro's knuckle ball for the Braves. It was Charlie Lau who observed one day in the bullpen, "There are two methods of catching the knuckle ball. And neither of them works." But it was Uecker who said, "The best way to catch a knuckle ball is to follow it until it stops rolling and then pick it up." Uecker went on the Johnny Carson show a while back and said, among other things, that "most people's bats say 'Powerized' down on the end. Mine said 'For Display Purposes Only.'" Uecker also does a little batting-practice pitching for the Braves, to keep loose, and on demand he will do imitations of various peculiar pitchers. "Dick Hall," someone will call out, and Uecker will go into a turkey-neck windup creditably like the original.

George Thomas, formerly of the Red Sox, is a man who was once told by former Boston manager Dick Williams, "George, you are just as funny on the field as you are off it." Once, in a spring exhibition game, when former teammate Joe Foy prepared to round third base against the Red Sox, he found that Thomas had removed and hidden third base. In 1970 both Thomas and the Phillies' Howard "Doc" Edwards were suddenly activated out of bullpen coaching jobs. Edwards disclosed that he had once qualified to ride Charlie Finley's mule in Kansas City. "He didn't have a blanket," said Edwards (in reference to the mule). "All he had on him was a satin cloth. And that wasn't cinched down. Well, a mule has no gait. The satin cloth started slipping, so I grabbed him around the neck. I slipped off and his forelegs nearly beat me to death. I got a standing ovation. That made two standing ovations in my career. The other was when I fell down going to the plate *with* my gear in Minnesota. I believe when you leave the dugout you ought to leave it running and hustling. Well, I tripped and fell across home plate."

Somehow we have come this far without mentioning Satchel Paige. It was he who said of the Williams shift, which was designed to

243

Earl Weaver: "Is that so?"

blockade the right-field side of the ball park against Ted Williams, "that thing took more gloves off first basemen than the end of the inning." Virtually everything else Paige has said has already been graven in stone, and rightly so. But when he was brought out of retirement by the Braves in 1968 and made an "assistant trainer" long enough to qualify for a five-year pension, he added an item to his legend one evening after a ballgame by getting into a police car parked outside the stadium and telling the driver to take him home. "When I'm out walking," the 62-year-old Paige remarked at one point during his brief revival, "people think I'm a young doctor. When they see Jackie Robinson with me they think I'm his son."

A great deal will undoubtedly die

Rodgers makes Chance laugh.

Dick Dietz?

out with Satchel Paige, assuming he ever dies out. But some old verities will live on. In the heat of the 1970 National League East race, the Pirates were either a hairbreadth in or a hairbreadth out of first place, and it was an hour and a half to game time in Atlanta. Pittsburgh trainer Tony Bartirome began to lay bets that he could lift three men at once.

"Hundred dollars," he was saying. "I can pick up any two men you pick, plus a third one I pick. As long as I can put the light one in the middle."

"Nah, you got a bad back," somebody said.

"Hundred dollars I can do it, I mean it."

Finally, after a great deal of discussion, Bartirome directed the two appointed heavy men, Willie Stargell and Dock Ellis, to lie flat on their backs on the floor and hook their arms and legs securely around those of one of the local clubhouse boys, who was slight.

Player Rep Dave Giusti got down close to the floor to be in a position to judge whether all three would indeed clear it at once.

"All right," said Bartirome,

evidently tensing himself for a great effort, "When I say 'Strain,' you strain.

"Strain."

With that he unzipped the completely immobilized clubhouse boy's trousers, and in a twinkling several Pirates had filled them to overflowing with shaving cream, soft drinks and sundry other liquids.

"Oh!" shouted an overjoyed Bob Moose. "We got to do that in Montreal! That French boy who can't speak English! He'll go 'Wallawallawalla . . .' He won't know *what* to say."

"That's an old clubhouse joke," explained Bartirome. "We did that to Bobby Del Greco and he said, 'I'm a thirty-year-old man. . . !' "

Yes, some of the old ways still hold up. However, modern club owners' and managers' intolerance toward drinking is cutting down on the volume of baseball humor. At least two big-leaguers were traded away following the 1970 season in large part because, just once or twice, they either came to work a little bit under the weather or

Warren Spahn in disbelief.

Frank Howard in ticklish situation.

failed to make it to work because they were a little bit over the weather. Rube Waddell would never have lasted eight years with the Athletics with that kind of attitude going around. Drinking has ruined a lot of ballplayers, of course, but it has also given us such stories as this one told by Kirby Higbe, the old Dodger pitcher, in his too-little-appreciated memoir, *The High Hard One:*

"Before a night game in St. Louis, four or five of us didn't get to the ball park until along about 7 o'clock, when we were supposed to be taking hitting practice. Dixie Howell, my roommate and the only catcher on the club that could handle the knuckle ball I had started to throw, still wasn't there. We were taking infield practice when Dixie showed up on the field, feeling fine. Preacher Roe was fielding throw-ins for the fungo hitter, and Dixie came charging onto the field and threw as good a flying tackle on him as I ever saw in a football game. Just having fun. When the game started, Dixie retired to the back of the dugout and went sound asleep.

"We went into the top of the seventh behind, 5–4. Billy took our pitcher out for a pinch hitter and told me to take Dixie to the bullpen and warm up. When he stepped out of the dugout, Dixie said, 'Roomie, it is really dark out here.' I told him to open his eyes."

Baseball, in many subtle ways, is becoming more sophisticated. One of those ways is not, obviously, humor. And that, to me, in some weird way, is a good thing.

José Tartabull and Rick Monday: acknowledging the applause?

They call that a hit in Detroit

official scoring

by Dick Young

To qualify for a position as "official scorer" you must be a
newspaperman and have covered at least 100 games a year for
three years. You must be willing to work for $35 a game. And
you must be part masochist. Dick Young meets these requirements
and as such is the author of the following section.

Mr. Young began his career at New York's *Daily News* at
age 18, as a messenger boy. He became a member of the Baseball
Writers Association in 1942. In 1946 he received his first "beat,"
the Dodgers. He has covered such moments as the first pennant
play-off in 1946, the suspension of Leo Durocher, the 1951 pennant
race and the breaking of the color line by Jackie Robinson.

The trim-bearded ballplayer threw a soiled towel angrily to the ground, mumbled something that sounded vaguely like "key-ryst!" then stormed up to the older man in the tall hat, the man standing near first base, and shouted: "How could you call that an error?"

It happened on June 19, 1846. It was on that day, at the Elysian Fields in Hoboken, New Jersey, that the first baseball game was played, and how could the first baseball game have been played without somebody, some ballplayer, second-guessing the official scorer?

Being human, the official scorer will, upon occasion, make a mistake, which in turn explains why he will be second-guessed. It is not necessary to be mistaken, however, in order to be second-guessed. Inasmuch as the function of an official scorer involves judgment (is it a hit or is it an error?), there is always the implicit invitation for the ballplayer to disagree.

There are written guidelines for scoring, but how do you put down in writing that which man must adjudge? Good shall prevail, says The Big Book, but as long as *you* think vanilla is good and *I* think vanilla is vomitous, it cannot be incontrovertibly written.

Scoring a ball game, therefore, is in the eyes of the beholder. Nobody can, with absolute precision, describe for you what is a hit and what is an error. I can tell you only how I do it. I cannot tell you it is the best way; I can tell you that I have found it best for me.

I employ a negative technique, a circuitous approach. I say to myself, "If the fielder had made the play, would it have been an unusually fine

play?" If the answer comes back *yes,* then I do not charge the man with an error. He is not required to make an unusually fine play. The words "with ordinary effort" recur in the official scorer's manual. That much is written.

My negative technique therefore combines judgment and the written word to produce—what? Infallibility? To produce that which one man believes to be proper and fair, based on his experience, his judgment, his bold integrity. Two men still may see the same play differently. The same man, on two successive days, may see virtually the same play differently. This is the human factor—to be lived with.

What makes me an official scorer? Somewhere in the convenient past it was decided by the leagues that qualified newspapermen should be the official scorers of baseball games. They had the first requisite: they were there. They were deemed qualified on the basis of extreme exposure to the sport. And they would work reasonably cheap.

The Baseball Writers Association of America (which calls itself the BBWAA under the mistaken idea that baseball is two words) has set up qualifications for scorers as follows: A reporter must have covered a minimum of one hundred games a year for three years to be eligible.

That is it. It might also help to insist that a scorer be color-blind, so as not to be able to distinguish between the colors of the home-team uniform and those of the visitor, but this is not required. Nor is the scorer asked to take an oath that he will not be a homer, a homer being one who favors, in his decision-making, members of the home club. It is simply presumed that he, like the umpire, is impartial.

However, a New York baseball writer scores only for games played in New York, a Chicago writer in Chicago, and so on. No city has a monopoly on objectivity, although the ballplayer in any city is convinced that the scoring for the

home team is more lenient (considerate?) in another town. A classic ballplayer-scorer exchange goes like this:

"They call that a hit in Detroit."

"I don't give a damn what they do in Detroit. It's an error."

"If a man doesn't get those kinds of hits at home, where can he get them?"

"A hit is a hit, no matter where, and an error is an error. Just because somebody else is a homer, don't ask me to be one."

Around and around we go. The player is convinced the scorer is out to get him; the scorer is convinced the player wants something for nothing, a bloody beggar.

Official scorers should not be influenced by the post-game persuasion of a hit-hungry ball-player, nor coerced by his anger. Neither should a scorer be so intractable as to be deaf to reasonable appeal. I do not mean appeal to his judgment, but occasionally a ball does take a bad hop that is not clearly visible at press-box level, or a throw does nick a man caught in a rundown just before the ball is dropped, and the true blame escapes the scorer.

There is one key word: blame. It is the essence of scoring. All too often, the official scorer becomes too technical, officious, a slave to the written rule. He will go thumbing through the pages of the manual looking for hidden meanings, seeking complications—and then one day, when the obscure play occurs, he will announce his gem triumphantly in the press box— instant expert.

Common sense is a better servant. Common sense serves the true duty of the official scorer, for what is his purpose? To reward the deserving; to blame those responsible. Thus two key words: reward, blame. Keeping those in mind, the scorer doesn't find himself trapped by technical verbiage.

Some years ago when a team

called the New York Giants played in a place called the Polo Grounds, somebody hit a high fly to left field, slightly toward center. It was a geographic peculiarity of the Polo Grounds that if the outfielders weren't careful they would step on one another. Thus, quite often, a man camped under a high fly would feel the warm breath of a colleague on his earlobe while hearing the encouragement, "You got it, old buddy."

In this particular case, the old buddy had it, then didn't have it. The ball hit into his glove and somehow curled out of it, fortunately on the side of the rooting teammate, who simply raised his glove and caught the evasive thing. The official scorer gave the ultimate fielder the put-out, which was fine, then added an assist for the juggler, which raised something of a stink in the press box and beyond.

"How in the world can you reward a man who has muffed a ball?" demanded the commonsense advocates.

"He touched the ball, didn't he?" said the official scorer, "therefore, he gets an assist," and no amount of dissuasion could convince him otherwise. Thus the undeserving left fielder was awarded an assist, just as surely as if he had thrown out a runner at the plate. (A footnote was later added to the scorers' manual, stating that "mere ineffective contact with the ball shall not be considered an assist.")

Periodically, displeasure over some outlandish scoring decision leads some fan to write a letter to the editor, or if the feelings are strong, to the league president, wondering why the duties of official

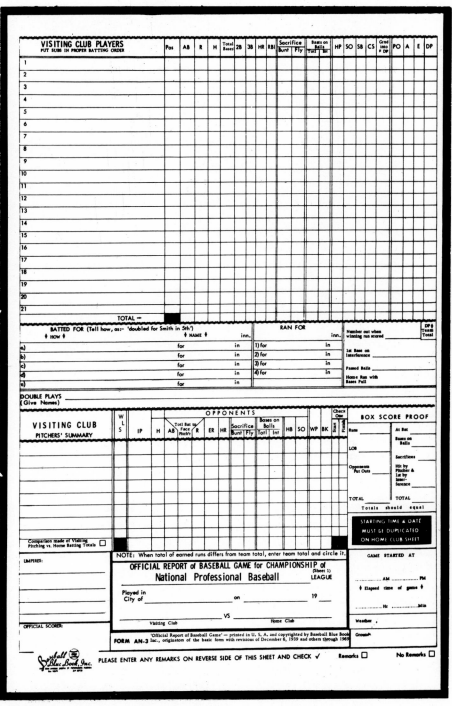

Official score sheet. Two sheets, one for the visiting club, one for the home team, are given to the official scorer. On reverse side of the home team sheet is a mass of instructions.

Yastrzemski and Smith collide—one will get an error.

receives, as a bonus, the gratis service of leading newspapermen on special committees. The constant review of scoring rules and statistical records, with an eye toward revision and modernization, is the function of such groups. At every meeting of the BBWAA such matters are debated openly—and beneficial change evolves.

The abolition of the free sacrifice bunt was the result of one of these get-togethers. Until a few years ago, any batter who advanced a runner with a bunt, regardless of the score or inning, was credited with a sacrifice and not charged with a time-at-bat if retired. This led to some very unsacrificial sacrifices. It was decided to give the official

scorer are not given to the umpire or perhaps to some overage ballplayer.

If the scorer were to be an umpire, he would have to be an added umpire, a fifth man who would sit at the press-box level, for a man on the field does not have the perspective to view all plays clearly. This would seem to be a good idea, with the fifth man rotating each day with the other four. However, such a man would be salaried at, say, $15,000, and his travel expenses would be roughly another $15,000. A twelve-team major league would require six such fifth men at an overall cost of $180,000. Put this alongside the $34,000 that the league now pays for scoring fees. And add the fact that there would be no guarantee of improved service to any degree, for the same human factors, the same variance of judgments and the same prejudices pertain to umpires as to reporter-scorers.

Official scorers are paid on a per-game basis. Since 1970, the major-league fee has been $35. This was part of the American inflationary spiral. The year before it was $30, and a few years prior to that, $25. As a rule, the eighty-one home games are divided among the newsmen regularly assigned to the ball club. Thus, in a two-newspaper city like Pittsburgh, each man will score forty or forty-one games, whereas in New York, four men do sixteen, one seventeen.

This is no grand lagniappe. In addition to making the calls, after each game the official scorer must fill out a statistical form and mail it to the league's sports bureau. The way modern managers throw the troops into battle, the official box score often takes longer to fill out than tax form 1040.

For the most part, newspapermen do not score only for the money. They do it for the participation, perhaps for the prestige. Baseball

scorer latitude. If common sense dictates that the batter obviously is bunting to get on base rather than to advance a runner (his team trailing 6–0 in the ninth inning), he shall be charged with a time-at-bat, regardless of the fact that a runner advances, and not credited with a sacrifice.

A giant stride forward in the scoring of games may be in the offing: the establishment of a team-error category. For years, scorers have been handicapped by the insistence that a specific fielder be charged with the error on a misplay that permits a man to reach base or to advance an additional base. There are several instances when this is patently unfair, when a play should have been made, but no one individual can be singled out as the culprit (fly ball lost in the sun; Alphonse-Gaston act by two fielders under pop fly; perfectly thrown ball that strikes sliding base runner, permitting further advance and so forth).

It is felt that the charging of an error to the offending team as a whole would serve the cause of justice by not rewarding pitchers with hits (and earned runs) they do not deserve and by not blaming fielders who might be blameless. There are, of course, opponents to the team-error concept, pure-thinking men who believe too much is being left to the scorer's judgment.

But is not all scoring judgment? Is that not the essence of an official scorer's prime duty—the exercise of judgment? There are some who contend that the latitude does not go far enough, that the taboo on misjudged balls and mental errors should be lifted, enabling the official scorer to say, and make it stick, "That ball should

251

Runner Mincher is safe while teammate strains for first. If only one of a possible two outs is made, no error is called.

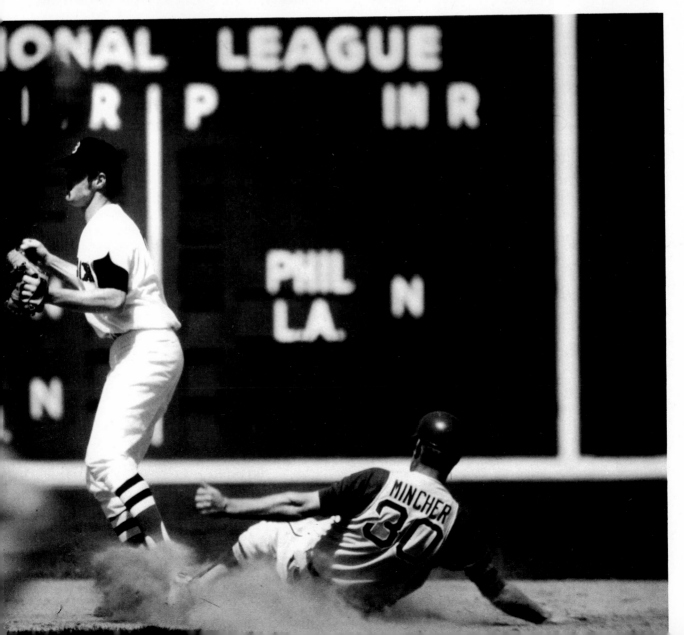

have been caught" or "That man would have been out had the pitcher covered first base."

Perhaps in time. For the present, judgment is restricted to some extent by the written word ("mental mistakes or misjudgments are not to be scored as errors . . ."), but there is steady progress.

Not that a degree of perfection will be reached that abolishes all controversy. Who could stand it? It would mean the end of baseball, death by sheer boredom. Argument is beautiful when concretely founded.

It should be emphasized that no official scorer can influence the outcome of a game. The scoring of a hit or an error in no way impedes or aids the advancement of a base runner. Such decisions belong only to umpires, and they can have it. The scorer can, however, influence the course of baseball history upon occasion, and has.

252   In 1923, a fine pitcher named Howard Ehmke, having been traded by Detroit to the Boston Red Sox, worked something of a miracle by winning 20 games for his new tail-end club. In the process, he pitched a no-hit game against the Philadelphia Athletics on September 7 and started next against the Yankees in New York.

The first batter to face him, Whitey Witt, sent a small bouncer toward third. The ball escaped the protruding hands of Howard Shanks, bounced abruptly upward and struck him in the chest while Witt raced safely to first.

Fred Lieb, the official scorer and a journalistic giant in his time, decreed it a hit for Witt. Not only was that the only hit by the Yankees

that day, but Witt was the only baserunner. As the game progressed and it became increasingly apparent that Ehmke was to be deprived of a second consecutive no-hitter because of the first-inning decision, extreme press box pressure was exerted on Lieb to alter his call.

The scorer held fast and when, sure enough, the game ended with only the questionable hit, friends of Ehmke petitioned the league president, Ban Johnson, to reverse the official scorer. Among the evidence present in support of Ehmke was an opinion by umpire Tommy Connolly that the ball should have been scored an error. Ban Johnson, to his credit, backed the official scorer. Thus it remained for Johnny Vander Meer, in 1938, to become the first pitcher (and the only one) to achieve successive no-hitters.

Fred Lieb also was involved in one of the most hectic batting-average disputes—on an occasion when, oddly enough, he was not the official scorer. At least he was not the *official* official scorer.

The year was 1922. Ty Cobb, the Detroit superstar, was in fierce battle with that inanimate rival, the .400 batting average. If he made it, it would be the third time for the fearsome Tyrus, a feat accomplished by only one man before him. Cobb finished with .401, but a tremendous outcry was raised against the figure's authenticity.

Crux of the dispute was a base hit credited to Cobb during a rainy midsummer game in New York. The

official scorer was John Kieran, then a baseball writer for the *New York Tribune,* subsequently a celebrity involved with such exercises as "Information Please," the original radio quiz show.

Cobb hit a ground ball in the vicinity of Everett Scott, Yankee shortstop. Kieran scored it an error. At that instant, the rain was driving into the exposed press section to the extent that Fred Lieb, covering for the *New York Press,* sought refuge in the covered grandstand to the rear. Over his shoulder as he fled, he glimpsed the play and hastily marked a base hit for Cobb in his scorebook.

You may ask why the opinion of Fred Lieb, the non-scorer, should overrule the judgment of John Kieran, the official scorer. Good question. In addition to

working for the *New York Press,* Lieb kept daily box scores for the Associated Press. Irwin Howe, head man of the American League's statistical bureau, located in Chicago, frankly admitted that, in tabulating Cobb's day-to-day batting average, he had used the AP box score for that day rather than the official score sheet eventually mailed to his office by John Kieran.

The one hit was important. Had Howe accepted Kieran's official version, Cobb would have finished with .399, not .401.

Irwin Howe said he deferred to Lieb on the basis of superior scoring experience, and Ban Johnson upheld that version. In New York, where Cobb was not exactly the most popular ballplayer alive, a furor erupted over The Case of the Two-Point Base Hit. The New York chapter of the Baseball Writers Association

Ball was thrown wide of second, forcing Petrocelli to come off base and allowing Tovar in safely. Error on the thrower.

brought it to the floor of the national BBWAA for a vote—the irony being that Lieb then was president of the BBWAA.

The Association voted against Lieb's version by a narrow margin, insisting that Cobb's average be recognized at .399. But the Reach and Spalding Baseball Guides for the following year carried it at .401. And so it stands today in all official records—an unofficial base hit.

It could not happen today. While it is possible for a league president to overrule a scorer on the matter of rule interpretation, it is unlikely he would second-guess the judgment of an official scorer. He certainly would not give precedence to an AP boxscore.

So while an official scorer cannot influence a game's outcome, he can influence something near and dear to the ballplayer—his personal record. Thus the occasional friction between player and scorer.

254

It must be remembered, however, that the ballplayer is not the most objective person involved in such matters, nor is the manager. This is why it is best for an official scorer to disregard the suggestion of a complaining ballplayer to "go ask Joe about it" —Joe being (a) a teammate, (b) the player on the other team who did not handle the ball or (c) the manager.

The apparent weakness in seeking such advice is that (a) the teammate is for his buddy, (b) the opposing player often will make a beau geste and (c) the manager invariably will take the side of his player, hopeful of ingratiating himself with all the players. There are many instances of managers waving a towel from the dugout toward the press box, or exhibiting some other form of histrionic criticism of a scoring decision, and there are cases on record of the league president warning, even fining, such a

manager for his unprofessional actions.

In a grand spirit of camaraderie, major-league ballplayers have been known to become similarly demonstrative, even physical. There was a case, not too many years ago, when a violent argument erupted around the Cincinnati batting cage over a scoring decision of the previous day. Oddly, the two men doing the most vociferous arguing had not been directly involved: the player was defending a viewpoint and a teammate, while the baseball writer supported the rule-interpretation of the scorer.

Things heated up to the point where the angered player took a halfhearted swing with the bat he

was holding, meaning to frighten the newsman, not hit him. But the bat struck a glancing blow on the shoulder. Bystanders were aghast, save one.

"Huh," snarled the struck newsman at the ballplayer who had been benched for poor hitting, "you even fouled me off."

Clockwise from above: Yaz dives
for line drive and misses—
no error; Joe Morgan takes a
perfect throw; Tony Perez
lets hard-hit grounder through.

255

Acknowledgment

The publisher wishes to thank the Office of the Commissioner of Baseball—
and of that office Joe Reichler.

Credits

The color photography and most of the black and white pictures
in this book were supplied by two photographers, Fred Kaplan and
Richard Raphael. Mr. Kaplan lives in San Rafael near San Francisco
and Mr. Raphael in Marblehead of the Boston area. The photographers
used a variety of motorized cameras and an assortment of lenses
ranging from f1.4 at 50mm to 1000mm telescopics.

Cover photos: by Fred Kaplan

Fred Kaplan: 2–3, 4–5, 37 right, 37 bottom, 38, 39 40 left, 40 bottom,
41, 42, 43, 44 left, 45, 46, 47, 50, 51, 55, 58, 59, 60–61, 63 top, 67,
69 right, 84, 113, 115, 116, 120, 121 left, 123 right, 165 upper right,
166–167, 168, 169, 170, 171, 172, 173, 177, 180, 181, 182, 183, 212 top,
213, 216, 217 bottom, 219, 222 right, 226, 227, 229 top, 229 left, 230
right, 231, 232 left, 233, 234, 235, 236, 238, 240, 241, 242, 243, 244,
245, 246, 248, 249, 250, 254, 255 top.

Richard Raphael: 1, 6, 7, 33, 34, 35, 36, 37 left, 40 right, 48, 53, 54
62, 63 bottom, 64, 65, 66, 68, 69 left, 71, 112, 118, 119, 122, 123 left,
165 (except upper right), 175, 176, 185, 186, 187, 189 top, 190, 191,
193, 194, 196, 197, 200, 206, 207 top, 208, 209, 212 bottom, 217 top,
221, 222 bottom left, 225, 230 left, 247, 251, 252–253..

Ken Regan: 44–45, 56–57, 123 center, 178–179, 220, 222 upper left.

Brown Brothers: 10–11, 12–13, 18–19, 20–21, 22–23.

Culver Pictures, Inc.: 16–17, 126, 127, 153 bottom.

Hall of Fame, Cooperstown, N.Y.: 9, 14–15, 125.

Houston Astros: 255 bottom.

Montreal Expos: 232 right.

New York Yankees: 229 right.

Underwood and Underwood: 132.

United Press International: 121 right, 128, 129, 131, 135, 137, 139, 140, 141, 143,
149, 150, 152, 153 top, 156, 157, 159 bottom, 161, 163.

Wide World Photos: 138, 147, 151, 155, 159.

Excerpt from *The High Hard One,* on page 245, by Kirby Higbe and Martin Quigley,
Copyright © 1967 by W. Kirby Higbe and Martin Quigley, All Rights Reserved,
reprinted by permission of The Viking Press, Inc.

Excerpt from *From Ghetto to Glory: The Story of Bob Gibson,*
by Bob Gibson and Phil Pepe, on pg. 83, reprinted by permission
of the copyright holder, Prentice-Hall.

Excerpt from *The American Diamond: A Documentary of the Game
of Baseball,* by Branch Rickey and Robert Riger, on pg. 188,
reprinted by permission of the copyright holder, Simon & Schuster.